SEEKING GOD

Poetic Devotions For a Life of Prayer

Tom Lemler

As God continues to give me poems, I attempt to be faithful in sharing them and allowing Him to use them for His purposes. This book includes a collection of original poems with some prayer points at the end of each poem to help guide you as you seek Him.

I pray that these poems are an encouragement and help to you as you journey through life. These writings are a reflection of my listening time with God. As I would pray and spend time with God, most of these simply appeared in my head complete and I simply found a keyboard or paper to collect the words together as they fell out of my head. I'm not real sure why He is giving me these now, other than to share, as I had lived over fifty years of life without anything like this coming out of my mind. I pray that God's gift to me is a blessing and help to you.

This book is dedicated in grateful acknowledgement to God, who has put these poems in my head and given me the ability to collect them.

In prayer,
Tom Lemler

All rights reserved. © 2014
ISBN 978-0-9916326-0-2

Tom Lemler
Impact Prayer Ministry
2730 S Ironwood Dr
South Bend IN 46614
www.impactprayerministry.com
tlemler@gapministry.com

Cover photo by MJ Lemler

Table of Contents

Battleground	6
Chaos	9
Childhood Joy	12
Christmas Reminder	15
Compassion	17
Differences	20
Elementary Christmas	22
Encouragement	24
The End	27
Everyone	30
Fanatic	33
Final Preparations	36
Fitness Training	38
Friends	40
God Cares	43
God's Way	45
Good Neighbor	48
The Greatest	50
Growth	53
Helpful Words	55

Table of Contents

Honesty	58
The Kings	61
Life's Journey	63
Listen	65
Listening Times	67
Living Hope	69
Mirror, Mirror	72
My Part	74
New Man	77
New Year's Opportunity	80
Opinions	82
Origins	85
Others	88
Our Mission	91
Overcomers	94
Overflow	96
Peace	99
Perception	102
The Prize	105
Practice	108

Table of Contents

Pure Religion	111
Refueling	113
Rest	116
Revival	119
Snow Days	122
Snowed In	124
The Source	126
Spring Thaw	128
The Story	130
Stuck	133
Survivor	136
Teamwork	138
Time With God	140
Trouble	143
Truth	145
Warnings	147
Why	150
Words	152
Work Day	154
Work In Progress	155

Battleground

I have a foe
that lives close to me.
So very close,
sometimes I don't see.
If I would just look,
it's not hard to find.
For this kind of foe
does live in my mind.
It hides in the corners
and lurks in the dark.
If I don't pay attention,
it sure leaves its mark.

Some of the enemies
I make on my own.
Others arrive from
some seeds that were sown.
My mind holds to memories,
both good and the bad.
And some that do linger,
will still make me sad.
The good's often hidden,
and kept out of sight.
The bad steps right up
and takes a big bite.

I see people talking
and think of the past.
My mind starts to wonder,
can these good times last?
I think there are people
who are much like me.
They have a hard time
living as free.
They've not felt much value,
they may be cast out.
They look o'er their shoulder,
and live with much doubt.

I know, for I've been there;
and still do reside.
With a mind that remembers
and keeps things inside.
God gives me these poems,
and He helps me to see.
That the things of the past,
today may not be.
The way people see me,
is not my concern.
My faith has more value
than what I do earn.

In times that are hard,
and jobs that did end.
I've always had present,
an eternal friend.
This friend that is with me,
is greater indeed.
Than all of my struggles,
and all of my need.
He's so much greater,
than I'll ever know.
He is the true One,
that has defeated my foe.

The power within me
is really my choice.
Do I listen to truth,
or the enemy's voice?
I have a promise,
that God Himself made.
Because He is with me,
I need not be afraid.
So when I have doubt
and fear moves on in.
I trust in my Savior,
for I know He will win.

God has blessed me greatly and He continues to help my faith to grow through reminders of some of what He has carried me through. I was thinking this morning about how far God has brought me and some of the struggles I still have and in the midst of this time with God, He gave me this poem. I pray that it encourages you to seek God when the foe in your mind wants to take charge.

Prayer Points

- Pray that you would have a clear mind that is constantly aware of the specific issues and circumstances that are most likely to cause you to be your own worst enemy.

- Pray that God's Spirit would guard your memories and refresh your mind so that the past would not haunt you as you pursue God today.

- Pray that you would be free of unfounded suspicions that would rob your daily life of the peace and joy that God desires to give you.

- Pray that God would show you the avenues He has provided for you to release the hurt from your past.

- Pray that your pursuit of God would keep you aware of His constant presence and of His power that is yours as you face the battles of the enemy.

- Pray that you would know God so well through your relationship with Him that you would easily distinguish between His voice and the voice of the enemy.

Chaos

There have been times,
I must confess.
I've made poor decisions,
creating a mess.
There are things that I've done
without giving much thought.
Then I've been surprised
by the chaos it wrought.
I stand in the rubble
and look all around.
And hope the path out
will someday be found.

Most people I know,
do like a routine.
If they know what is coming,
they won't cause a scene.
If they're pointed out
and put on the spot.
Look out and run fast,
they're bound to be hot.
But there are a few
who like a surprise.
Last minute changes,
just help them to rise.

If you're one or the other,
or somewhere between.
If you want to be hidden,
or like to be seen.
If you walk in the middle,
with a foot in each camp.
When we understand others,
we turn on a lamp.
The lamp is revealing
and helps us to see.
People may not be wrong
that are different from me.

The connection is coming,
if there's one to this poem.
The message is clear,
it's about to hit home.
When we judge others
by the rules that we make.
We create chaos,
because God's rules we break.
There is just one standard,
that applies to us all.
When held up to Jesus,
every person will fall.

When I make decisions,
what will be my guide?
Will I open my motives,
and have nothing to hide?
Will I base them all solely,
on God and His Word.
So it is His message
that always is heard.
When I trust in Jesus
and follow His path.
Even when I caused it,
I escape from His wrath.

I guard my words closely,
and capture each thought.
So His Spirit helps me,
only say what I ought.
To give a quick answer,
can be trouble for me.
So I spend time in prayer,
even down on my knee.
To make this a habit,
does not make me weak.
I am much stronger,
when God's face I seek.

I was tempted to comment on several posts and statements that I've read this morning that I simply don't agree with and think are bad conclusions to the known information. As I was considering what to write, God gave me this poem instead as a reminder that being quick to speak/respond often leads me into chaos. I pray that this poem is an encouragement to you and that it brings glory to God and accomplishes His purposes for it.

Prayer Points

- Pray that God would help you to see how your decisions have contributed to your current circumstances.
- Pray that God would fill you with His hope regardless of your circumstances.
- Pray that you would learn to trust God completely through times that catch you by surprise.
- Pray that God would help you to see value in godly habits and practices that may seem routine to you.
- Pray that you would be a person who spends time in God's Word for the purpose of knowing God and how He would have you to live.
- Pray that God's Word would not only be your measuring stick, but that it is what you use in your view of others.
- Pray that your words to, and about, others would reflect God's design of their life and not simply be a statement of how you feel about them.

Childhood Joy

Some time ago
when I was a boy.
The simplest things
would bring me great joy.
It didn't take much
to fill up my time.
I'd work on the farm
or play in the slime.
It didn't matter
if work or if play.
Being a family
had value each day.

We did not have much
but we had each other.
My brothers and sister,
my dad and my mother.
We worked really hard,
we played just the same.
We even decided
chores could be a game.
The things that we lacked,
I could not even tell.
We had what we needed,
we really lived well.

The things that we had
that many did lack.
Was a house full of love
and even some slack.
I always had value,
even when I did wrong.
In my own family
I would always belong.
I cannot imagine
how different I'd feel.
If my growing up
was anything but real.

Now I fast-forward
through quite a few years.
Years full of blessing
and even some tears.
And while I am wiser
or older, at least.
Sometimes the joy's gone,
eaten up by the beast.
You may never see it
but the beast is out there.
Stealing contentment,
thinking no one will care.

I'm not all that different
from days long ago.
Joy fills my life
through the people I know.
The value they give me
by what they do say.
Is the mark of a good friend,
in work and in play.
I pray that these lessons,
I learned as a boy.
Would lead to contentment
and fill you with joy.

As I was spending time with God, reflecting on joy and contentment, He reminded me that I often look for both of those in all the wrong places. We are often taught in so many ways that the stuff we accumulate should bring us great joy. When joy doesn't come we may decide we simply need more stuff. God took me back to my childhood that was filled with great joy even though we didn't have a lot of possessions. It is a lesson I need to be reminded of often and I pray that it is a reminder that is helpful to you.

Prayer Points

- Pray that God would help you to understand His continual presence in bringing you to where you are in life today.

- Pray that you would be able to see the pure joy that can be found in the simple things of life.

- Pray for those people that God has used in your life to be your family and for those who have shown you a glimpse of His family.

- Pray for those around you, perhaps even yourself, who do not experience the love of a family. Pray that God's people, perhaps even you, would help to fill the gaps and voids of the missing family.

- Pray that God would help you to find joy in the work that you do. Pray for an understanding of the good work He has created for you to do.

- Pray that you would understand more fully, and share with others, the great value that we have in God's sight that Jesus would die for us while we were still in sin.

- Pray that you would be the kind of friend and family member that spreads joy and contentment to all who are in your life.

- Pray for the people that you know who are caught up in materialism, thinking they can somehow find joy in a multitude of possessions.

Christmas Reminder

Christmas is here,
the day's finally come.
When people will gather
for good family fun.
As you come to dinner
and pull up your seat,
There are people are out there
who have nothing to eat.
You have two choices,
what to do with that news.
Sharing with others
is the one that I choose.

God tells us clearly
to help those in need.
But often I fail to
because of my greed.
I need reminded
to care for the weak.
To stand up and speak out
for those who can't speak.
It doesn't take long
to notice out there,
Someone who's hurting,
then show them you care.

To visit the lonely
and care for the sick,
Give food to the hungry,
and the message might stick.
It's all about doing
what God said is best.
To hear Jesus tell you,
"Enter into my rest!"
I pray that this Christmas
you'll clearly see,
Hope is for everyone,
not just you and me!

I pray that you consider the words of Jesus in Matthew 25:31-46 this Christmas as you celebrate the birth of Jesus. His birth, death, burial, and resurrection was meant to be good news for all the people! What are you doing to make that good news known?

Prayer Points

- Pray that your eyes would always be open to the people around you who lack food, clothing, and shelter.

- Pray that God would fill you with compassion and create within you a desire to help people who are in need.

- Pray for a softening of your heart toward others and a spirit of generosity that rightly considers God's ownership of all the resources you manage.

- Pray for wisdom and a discerning spirit to know what is actually helpful to those in need and to not be drawn into perpetuating the need.

- Pray for the people around you who are in need, that they would be open to hearing and accepting the good news of Jesus because of your care and concern.

- Pray for the humility needed so you can help others without demeaning them.

- Pray for the courage to do what God wants you to when it comes to the lonely, sick, and hungry.

Compassion

When life seems all wrong
and nothing's the same.
Most of the time
we want someone to blame.
We look all around
for who it could be.
I guess it is you
'cause it sure isn't me.
Yet when we step back
and see that isn't true.
We look up above
and say, "God, I blame you."

I have seen this happen,
it might have been me.
It's not that unusual,
I think you'll agree.
When we're in the midst
of what we don't understand.
It's hard to imagine
that it all turns out grand.
One of the problems
when we start to blame God.
We step away from
His comforting rod.

If you are wondering
from where did this come.
It happened this morning
before the rising sun.
It was a big seizure,
this I do know.
The pain and the anger
needed somewhere to go.
The mind was not thinking
as it normally would.
So it lashed out in anger
at everyone that it could.

There wasn't just anger,
there was also remorse.
Back and forth it would go,
driven along by some force.
For seizures do seize,
that's what they do best.
They take full control
and then no one gets rest.
While it is not pretty
to watch and endure.
Living like this
is much harder, I'm sure.

Then comes a moment
when the mind starts to click.
"I really do need help
for I am so sick."
And it didn't matter
whether angry or sad.
Our love was still given
because we're mom and dad.
We do what we can do
and pray for the best.
And know there's a day
that we all will find rest.

In case you are wondering,
about all of this.
I pray that you're listening
and the point you don't miss.
We all have our moments
when we're out of control.
We really need someone
who can help make us whole.
That will come and just hold us,
and quietly say.
"My child I am with you,
with you I will stay."

As I was praying for my daughter, Susan, following a major early morning seizure, this poem showed up in my mind so I collected it to share. Many times, I think that Susan's seizures give me insight into God's immense love and compassion for us when we are seized by the control of selfishness, desire, substances, sin, and the evil one. We often lash out at God and even in the midst of our lashing out, He is trying to draw us near to comfort and protect us. I pray that this poem helps you in your pursuit of God and in your letting God make you whole when something that is not of Him has seized your life.

Prayer Points

- Pray that God would fill you with a spirit of patience when things go wrong and you want someone to blame.

- Pray for the courage to consider what might be going on "behind the scenes" when it appears someone has wronged you.

- Pray that you would more clearly recognize the times when the enemy takes control of a situation and attempts to use it to divide and conquer.

- Pray that the people around you today would hear from you about the God who loves them.

- Pray for a spirit of compassion to help you comfort the frightened people around you whose lives seem to be out of their control.

Differences

I like to drink coffee
from my favorite cup.
I add creamer and flavoring,
then I fill it right up.
A couple of soft mints
and ice cream is good.
But I still call it coffee,
do you think that I should?
While I like to add things,
some others do not.
They won't call mine coffee,
even though it is hot.

There are some people
who are living out there.
They'll take such a difference
and let me know they care.
That's not how they like it,
so I must be wrong.
If I don't agree
then I do not belong.
While all this sounds silly,
it happens too much.
When we disagree
about style and such.

I'm not really writing
about coffee per se.
But things that divide us
almost every day.
Most of the issues
that we try to face.
Would disappear quickly
if we're in the right place.
That place is not distant,
very close I would say.
It's wherever we are
when we start to pray.

So as I drink coffee
that's all full of stuff.
Be happy I like it,
don't get in a big huff.
This gentle reminder
is not just for you.
For I need to value
the things that you do.
When all that is different
is made into one.
The unity created
will look like the Son!

I came in from running the snow blower and clearing walks and as I made a cup of coffee, this poem appeared in my head. No, I didn't have ice cream in the coffee tonight but I did have vanilla caramel creamer, caramel coffee syrup, and two soft mints in it and it was delicious. I pray that this poem is an encouragement and help to you so that when differences appear large, you would remember to pray.

Prayer Points

- Pray that you would better appreciate the differences in people as you realize that being different is not always about being right or wrong.

- Pray that you would learn to give and receive grace in the matters of opinion that you hold.

- Pray the prayer of Jesus that all of His followers would be one just as He and the Father are one.

Elementary Christmas

'Twas the week before Christmas
and all through the schools.
Not a student was listening
nor following the rules.
Their minds were all elsewhere
and thinking with joy.
That Christmas might bring them
the latest new toy.

Then quite unexpected
and out of the blue.
The meaning of Christmas
came shining right through!
They sang of sweet Jesus
and remembered His birth.
That very first Christmas
when God came to earth.

It was quite a lesson
I pray we did learn.
The real gift of Christmas
was given, not earned.
These lines are over,
the rhyming is done.
My prayer for each person,
that we'd follow the Son!

I pray that you find some joy and encouragement through these words. I've not even made an attempt at writing a poem since high school English when I was required to. Yet as I considered the school and preschool children that are in the building every day as I work, these lines just flowed from my mind. I figure that God put them there and He brought them out, so He has a purpose to use them in someone's life. I pray that someone is you!

Merry Christmas!

Prayer Points

- Pray that the importance of the birth of Jesus would be remembered for what it is each day of your life.

- Pray that you would not be distracted by the commercialization of religious occasions, but would use them as opportunities to speak of the real message of the Bible.

- Pray that you would have a greater recognition of the incredible value of God's gift to you.

- Pray that you would always remember that God's mercy and grace expressed to mankind is a true gift — there is nothing you could ever do to earn any of it.

- Pray that you would have a child-like heart that can see and accept the innocent joy found in the birth of Jesus.

- Pray that you would consider how God would have you to use the gifts He has given you, then pray for the courage and boldness to use them for that purpose.

- Pray for the people around you who do not have an understanding of the importance of Jesus coming to earth. Pray that they would hear and see from you the clear message of the hope you have because of your life in Christ.

Encouragement

Do not be afraid
but take courage now.
It's a message from God
yet we wonder how.
Sometimes life is full
of things that cause fear.
We're so overwhelmed
that God we don't hear.
We should not be alone
when we are afraid.
We have His Spirit
and the friends we have made.

Sometimes we forget
the friends God will give.
He puts them around us
to help as we live.
A cord of three strands
is not easily broken.
It's not only true,
it's what God has spoken.
Everyone needs help
when we get knocked down.
To pick us up gently
and straighten our frown.

It is a good thing
when we have each other.
To carry the load
as sister and brother.
When one who is weak
is helped by the strong.
It gives us great hope
that we all do belong.
Sometimes we're strong
and sometimes we're not.
It shouldn't matter
if a good friend we've got.

To carry a burden
as if it's our own.
Is a godly result
of the seed that was sown.
My life's not an island,
I don't live it alone.
When friends do surround me,
each other we hone.
As we sharpen each other
at work and at play.
We look more like Jesus
each and every day.

So what's growing in you
as you look around?
Will you pick up a brother
when he's on the ground?
To help those who help you,
is only a start.
To love the forgotten,
you must open your heart.
And as your heart opens
to let others in.
God's courage will fill you
and a victory you'll win.

Before fear takes over
and courage does end.
Take a good look around
at who you call friend.
This may be a time
when they really need you.
It's also a time
when you need them too.
So when fear arrives
take a good look above.
And thank God for friends
who show you His love.

I attended a ministers' prayer time and fellowship this morning that I am privileged to be a part of. As I was thinking about the encouragement I receive from these guys, as well as the Deer Run congregation, I was praying that God would use me to encourage them as much as they encourage me. As I was praying, God put this poem in my mind to share. I pray that it encourages you and brings glory to God.

Prayer Points

- Pray that you would seek courage through your relationship with Jesus.

- Pray that you would experience God's peace that surpasses all understanding during the times that you feel overwhelmed by the things in your life.

- Pray that God would surround you with friends who will encourage you when you are down.

- Pray that you would be a friend to those around you who need encouragement.

- Pray that God would open your eyes to the hurting people that are already in your life.

- Pray that God would fill you with compassion for the needy that surround you each day.

- Pray that your relationships with others would reflect on a daily basis the encouragement you have received from being united with Christ.

The End

I took time today
to visit a friend.
He has been told
his life will soon end.
The thing that I thought
as we took time to chat.
We don't like to think,
"Am I ready for that?"
We'd much rather keep
pretending each day.
That nothing could happen
to take life away.

When we stop to think
that this day could be it.
Does it change what we do
with the times we just sit?
To reflect on our life
that God Himself gave,
We should recognize
that we need Him to save.
There's only two choices
at the end of this life.
Forever with Jesus,
or eternal strife.

Do I live each day
like it could be my last?
Long for the future
with a forgiven past?
Will people surround me
with stories of good?
Will they say I loved Jesus,
like I said that I would?
And if I do wonder,
just what they might say.
A pretty good answer,
is what's said today.

So how will I live,
this day to the full?
Will I draw near to Jesus
as my heart He does pull?
Will I think more clearly
than ever before?
And realize without Him,
I'm way beyond poor.
He's the great treasure
that I have received.
His Spirit has filled me
because I believed.

Because of His presence,
it's really okay.
If quite unexpected,
this is my last day.
But if He should give me
a little more time.
I pray that He's seen,
in my life and my rhyme.
I want to be faithful
in all I do spend.
So He says, "Welcome home,
it's not really the end."

I spent some time yesterday with a friend who has outlived his doctor's expectation but knows he is nearing the end of his life on this earth. Because they fit him, he is ready for those words, "Well done, good and faithful servant." As I've been praying for him and his wife, God put this poem in my mind. I pray that it helps each of us to spend time with God considering if we are ready for this journey on earth to end.

Prayer Points

- Pray that God would open your eyes to those around you that are nearing the end of life on this earth.

- Pray that God's Spirit would help you to examine where you are in your relationship with God.

- Pray that you would consider if there are specific good works that God prepared in advance for you to do.

- Pray that God would help you to see if there is still unfinished business that you have in your relationship with Him, or with others.

- Pray that your life is being lived in such a way that as your life nears its end, people would surround you with stories of how your faithfulness has made a difference in their life.

- Pray that God would help you to recognize the brevity of life so that you would live today exactly as you would want to if you knew for certain it would be your last.

- Pray that your longing for the things of eternal value would motivate you to help others be ready for the time their life on earth will end.

- Pray that the people around you would see Jesus represented well in the way you live, talk, and listen.

Everyone

I am part of a group
to which I belong.
It is not for those others,
for their lives are lived wrong.
I do take for granted
all the good things I've got.
Don't ask me to share them,
of course I will not!
It is easy to think
I deserve all these things.
Don't blame me for their lack,
they just got what life brings.

The good news of Jesus
is for people like me.
To spread it much further,
that just shouldn't be.
I hope that you're thinking
as you're reading this poem.
The lights may be on
but there's nobody home.
The truth is much different
than these lines that I wrote.
Like it or not,
we are in the same boat.

As you consider
the way it might seem.
When put down on paper,
this view is extreme.
But when you look deeper
at the things that you do.
Could this type of thinking
exist in you too?
If you think that can't happen,
then you'll need to meet.
A good man named Peter
and an animal filled sheet.

Peter was godly,
he did what was right.
But there were some people
that he kept out of sight.
They're just not like us,
I'm not being mean.
For we are God's chosen
and they are unclean.
So God spoke to Peter
when he went to pray.
They're all my creation,
they're clean if I say.

Peter did realize
the message God sent.
When the "unclean" did call him
he got up and he went.
To a man named Cornelius,
he brought the good news.
To all who would seek Him,
God gladly would choose.
The lesson forgotten
again and again.
We all need God's mercy
when it comes to our sin.

Before you quit reading,
dismissing all of this.
The message is for you,
no one does it miss.
There's only one reason
you have a great hope.
It's not that you're so good,
to that, God says nope.
Unmerited favor,
this thing we call grace.
Yes, it is for you,
and the whole human race.

So do you remember
how this poem began?
To make you think, "crazy",
was part of the plan.
Sometimes our actions
need to be put in print.
To see them more clearly,
or at least get a hint.
So when you see others,
you think don't belong.
Remember God's mercy
and admit you are wrong.

As I was spending time with God praying and going through Acts 11 for a sermon I plan to share tomorrow, this poem appeared in my mind. I pray that God uses it as He chooses and that each of us would notice the people that we have a tendency to ignore and that we would choose to find ways to share Jesus with them instead.

Prayer Points

- Pray that God would help you to see the value of people who are not exactly like you.

- Pray that all of the people around you would see and hear a message of hope in Jesus from you.

- Pray that God would help you to see any areas of exclusion or indifference you have toward groups of people.

- Pray that you would always extend the same grace and mercy that you have received from Jesus to all of the people around you.

Fanatic

So many people
will root for their team.
They'll stand up and cheer
as quite loudly they scream.
They don't even care
if you like it or not.
They'll tell you all day
their team is so hot.
The more you object,
the louder they are.
Their team is the best,
of course they'll go far.

Fanatics they are,
but don't call them that.
They'll wear their team's shirt,
a coat and a hat.
They'll speak out quite boldly
and get in your face.
If you even think
that their team's second-place.
Standing together
or standing alone.
They'll share their allegiance,
a text to your phone.

You may not like it,
they don't even care.
Nothing will stop them
when they want to share.
They won't be too timid
or silenced by fear.
Their team is the greatest
and this you must hear.
They'll spend all their money
and sacrifice much.
Their time is all given
so that they stay in touch.

I think this sounds normal
and really not odd.
Until we start talking
of a "team" led by God.
Then all of a sudden
the story does change.
We make up our reasons
and excuses arrange.
I can't cheer for Jesus,
I won't be that loud.
It wouldn't be right,
standing out in the crowd.

I must be real careful
in all that I say.
Some may not like it
if I say there's one way.
No one can notice,
I won't make a wave.
Speaking for Jesus
belongs to the brave.
Yes, I know Jesus
is the Lord of my life.
But I want to keep silent
and avoid all the strife.

So what good could happen
and who could we reach?
If a passion for Jesus
is something we'd teach?
If all the fanatics
in all of the stands.
Would rise up for Jesus
and cover the lands.
If sharing the gospel
wherever we went.
Was worth all the effort
and whatever was spent.

To raise up a family
of fanatics for God.
It could be effective
even if it seems odd.
To stand up and speak out,
to cheer on His name.
To make sure all people
know this isn't a game.
As you consider
who is number one.
I pray that you realize
it's Jesus, God's Son!

I caught parts of the football playoff games today and it made me think of the extreme efforts many will go to in support of a sports team. As I was reflecting on that and seeing my newsfeed fill with various claims of greatness on behalf of the different teams that were still playing, this poem showed up in my mind. I pray that our enthusiasm and fervor for things in life would always be overshadowed by our passion for God.

Prayer Points

- Pray that you would never be ashamed to stand up and speak out for Jesus.

- Pray that Jesus would receive your full support in the way you talk, live, and use the resources that you manage.

- Pray that you would be willing to "go all out" for the cause of sharing the gospel everywhere that God would take you.

Final Preparations

If you knew that this year
was the last you would get.
Would you be more active
or quietly sit?
Would you talk more of Jesus
and tell the good news?
Or keep to yourself,
which one will you choose?
If this is the year
that Jesus will come,
Will you be ready,
will He say, "Well done!".

If you're not too sure
of what He would say,
I ask you to listen
and seek Him today.
He gives us the truth
throughout His good Book.
So why don't you sit down
and take a good look.
If we read His story
from beginning to end.
We'll see His desire is
to call us His friend.

So how should you answer
and what should you do,
If this is the year
Jesus comes for you, too.
Ask Him to cleanse you
and wash away sin.
Love and serve others,
their soul seek to win.
And if you should wonder
how God you could please.
Then feed, clothe, and visit
all who are "least of these".

If you should ask me
just what does that mean.
I'll point you to Jesus
as He shares a scene.
He tells us a story
of quite a large crowd.
Some are cast out to
a place that is loud.
The only real difference
as He made His choice,
Were they serving others –
the ones with no voice.

As I was praying for a couple of families who have lost loved ones in the past week, God opened up this poem in my mind and out it came. I pray that these words are a help and encouragement to you as you consider your readiness for the Lord's return.

Prayer Points

- Pray that you would have the courage and wisdom to live each day as if it were your last.

- Pray that you would examine scripture and your relationship with God to see if you are ready for the return of Jesus.

- Pray that your understanding of God's Word would make you a "doer" of His Word and not just a "hearer".

- Pray that the people around you today would understand the importance of a relationship with Jesus in order to be ready for their final day.

Fitness Training

To get into shape,
I thought I would try.
So I packed up my bag
and I went to the Y.
When I did get there,
to the pool I did go.
The hot tub was pleasant,
the swimming, so-so.
I swam one whole pool length
and then I swam back.
They said to keep going
then I might get on track.

So I kept on going
but I'm pretty sure.
Not all of me liked it,
what I had to endure.
A life that's been easy
for most of a year.
Has been hard on my body,
of that I do fear.
So I'll keep on going,
I won't let it rest.
Then my level of fitness
will be at its best.

As I do consider
the shape that I'm in.
Something's more important
than if I'm fat or I'm thin.
My soul's great deep longing,
its searching for God.
I work on it daily
as I'm walking this sod.
My heart's big desire
is God I would know.
That His presence lives through me
wherever I go.

As I keep working
so I'll be more fit.
Part of my routine
is with God I'll just sit.
To condition the body
and exercise well.
Has a noticeable value
that most people can tell.
And my spiritual training,
I really do pray.
Makes my life look like Jesus
each and every day.

I went to the Y today to work on my physical condition and God placed this poem in my mind as I spent time with Him working on my spiritual condition. I pray that His name is glorified through my life and that these words help you in your pursuit of a vibrant relationship with God through His Son, Jesus.

Prayer Points

- Pray that God would help you to find the proper balance that He would desire for you in the care of a physical body that is not eternal.

- Pray that the value you place on physical training would not overshadow the greater value of spiritual training.

- Pray that the fruit of God's Spirit would be more evident in your life each day as you spend time training with God.

Friends

When a good friend is sad
and feeling all blue.
Most of the time,
we're not sure what to do.
We want to be helpful
and not cause more pain.
We're not too sure how,
so to help we refrain.
The problem is thinking,
the pain we must cure.
Sometimes just listening
will help them endure.

This problem's not new,
in fact it's quite old.
Read the story of Job
if you're feeling that bold.
He had much more loss
than anyone should.
His friends tried to help
as any friend would.
They had a good start,
as at first they just sat.
But it didn't take long,
to give up on that.

Their next course of action
was some questions to ask.
To figure it all out,
they took as their task.
There must be a reason
for all of this loss.
He must have done something
to offend the big "Boss".
We know the ending
and also the start.
The story's much bigger,
they only saw part.

The same may be true
as we help a friend.
Always remember,
you can't see the end.
Some things you may notice
as they walk their road.
But you won't see it all,
so help carry their load.
You don't need to solve it,
or have the right word.
You just need to be there,
so they know they are heard.

So how do you help them,
the friends who are sad?
Be a good listener
and the best friend they've had.
Help them remember
the times from before.
When God has been with them,
He's opened the door.
And point to the future
where God always is.
And remind them so gently,
that they are still His.

Here's another poem that came out of my prayer time for a friend. I pray that it helps each of us to remember to be the friend we would want to have.

In prayer,
Tom

Prayer Points

- Pray that God would help you to be observant to the needs of your friends.

- Pray that you would become a better listener as you spend time with people who are hurting and in need.

- Pray that you would be careful not to take on the task of fixing something that you know nothing about and is not yours to fix.

- Pray that God would help you to become the kind of friend that you would want to befriend you.

- Pray that you would seek to help carry the burdens of your friends rather than blame them for having burdens.

- Pray that the people around you today would experience a true friendship that is empowered by your relationship with Jesus.

- Pray that you would be able to understand when your friends need someone to "weep with those who weep" and when they need someone to cheer them up.

- Pray that your life would be an encouragement to others of how God has given you hope and comfort in the midst of your times of sadness and despair.

God Cares

The squirrels are all playing
in the midst of the trees.
The birds' song is carried
along in the breeze.
As I sit and ponder
all that's out there.
I'm always reminded
that my God, He does care.

Sometimes I wonder
if a difference I make.
As I seek to serve others
all for His great name's sake.
As I'm using my talents
and attempting some good,
it's so very easy
to be misunderstood.

That shouldn't matter
if this is my aim.
God calls me to faithfulness
not world-wide fame!
And so I get busy
in doing some good.
In sharing of Jesus
as He says I should!

I pray that you find some encouragement in these words. As I was noticing the squirrels and birds outside my office window, it was a great reminder of the care God has for His children. It was also quite amazing how quickly these words found their way out of my head and through the keyboard to my computer screen.

In prayer,
Tom Lemler

Prayer Points

- Pray that God would help you to notice each day how He cares for the things we often think are small or insignificant.

- Pray that God would use you to encourage others to recognize the care that God has for them.

- Pray that God would open your eyes and heart to how He would have you show His care for the people around you.

- Pray that you would guard your mind against measuring God's care for you by the materialistic standard the world likes to use.

- Pray that the people around you today would know, and believe, God's care for them as an individual.

- Pray that you would understand, and practice, the greatest care that you can show to a person is to share with them the message of salvation found in Jesus Christ.

- Pray that God's favor would rest upon you as you live a life of faithfulness in sharing of God's love and care to others.

- Pray that you would not become discouraged when people misunderstand your efforts of sharing God's care with them.

God's Way

Words seem so empty
when friends have great hurt.
If it would help them,
I'd give them my shirt.
We plan and we dream
and we work really hard.
When our dreams are shattered
we get cut by the shard.
While the wound isn't open
with blood rushing out.
The hurt is as painful
and we want to shout!

We sit and we wonder,
we've waited so long.
How in the world
did things go so wrong.
The days have no answers
the nights creep on past.
The hurting continues,
how long will it last.
Then we start to question,
when life's so unfair.
What have I done, so
that no one would care?

In these long moments
and miserable days.
It's very important
that I change my gaze.
Looking within me
is a good place to start.
To examine my motives
and clean up my heart.
To change what needs changin'
from inside to out.
And do it completely
to leave room for no doubt.

When I have examined
all that's inside.
I lift up my head,
I have nothing to hide.
I look back with sorrow
at what was back there.
Then look up to heaven
to feel His great care.
It's in this here moment
that I understand.
My God did not cause this,
He is holding my hand.

So what am I saying
and what have I learned?
In the midst of rejection
when I feel so spurned.
Whether it's my fault
or the fault of some man.
God's not left wondering,
He still has a plan.
It may not be better
as people will say.
But it will be good,
for that is God's way.

I wrote this poem . . . or more accurately, this poem fell out of my head in about ten minutes as I was praying for some friends who are going through a difficult time. Difficult times are never pleasant — that's why they're called difficult times — but they can help us grow strong in faith and compassion. I pray that whatever difficult times you find yourself in, that you would allow God to strengthen and comfort you so that you can be used to strengthen and comfort others.

Prayer Points

- Pray that God would fill you with compassion to help you not be a dispenser of empty words when the people around you experience hurt.

- Pray that you would recognize and have an understanding of the "invisible" hurt people experience.

- Pray that you would have the courage to look to God first during times of great hurt.

- Pray that the hurt you experience would motivate you to make any changes that God would say is necessary.

- Pray that you would recognize and feel God's presence with you in the midst of suffering.

- Pray that the people around you today who are hurting would experience the comfort of God's presence through His children.

- Pray that you would continually learn to trust God to make all things — even pain and suffering — work to accomplish good as you fulfill His purposes.

- Pray that you would give, and receive, a message of hope and comfort in times of trouble.

- Pray that these words reach all who God purposed them to touch.

Good Neighbor

As I sit and ponder
the things Jesus taught.
I like to consider
that I do what I ought.
About His commandments,
if the point He should raise.
Would I say I have followed
them all of my days?
To care for my neighbor
as He says I should.
Would I ask who that is,
thinking I'm pretty good?

Jesus tells us a story
of a man just like me.
He lived a good life
but he wanted to see.
So he went to ask Jesus
and to Him he did call.
Which of the commandments
is the greatest of all?
Jesus turned it back to him,
the question he sought.
And the man answered rightly
with what he'd been taught.

But the man wasn't happy
with the answer he got.
So he raised a new question,
who's a neighbor, who's not?
Jesus tells him a story
of a man who is hurt.
He is beat up and robbed,
left to die in the dirt.
The "good" folks do pass him
as they make their path wide.
Then a Samaritan helps him
and gives him a ride.

At the end of the story,
Jesus turns the question around.
Who was the neighbor
to the man on the ground?
As the man answers Jesus,
the point he does get.
The one that's a neighbor
made sure needs were all met.
So what will you do
when you think you're that good?
Will you live like a neighbor
to all as you should?

I've been praying lately about my response to situations and seeking wisdom in giving proper responses, not ones simply designed to justify myself. This poem came from a combination of those prayer times and the time I'm spending in the gospel of Luke for the sermon series I am preaching. I pray that this ministers to you in the way God desires for it to.

Prayer Points

- Pray that God would help you to accurately evaluate how you are doing at living according to His Word.

- Pray that you would always submit to the instructions of Jesus rather than trying to justify yourself before Him.

- Pray that you would be more concerned about being a good neighbor than having a good neighbor.

The Greatest

They say life's about
just how high you can reach.
At least that is what
many do like to teach.
We claw and we scrape,
climb our way to the top.
There's no way on earth
that we ever will stop.
The fittest survive,
the strong beat the weak.
Top place in this order
is all that we seek.

We collect many people
for what we can use.
When they ask for our help
we do quickly refuse.
I'd like to help you,
really, I would.
But I'm very sorry,
this is all for my good.
A method exists
to our madness you see.
You can be my friend
if it's all about me.

We pick and we choose
who's deserving, who's not.
All the while looking
at what all they've got.
People are equal
according to law.
Yet our favoritism
creates a huge flaw.
Justice is blind,
at least that they say.
But somehow it sees
just how much you can pay.

To the Good Book I go
to see about this.
I look and I look
because something's amiss.
To use up good people
so I get my way.
Is so set against
the way Jesus did pray.
He asked of the Father
to help all of us.
To spend our life serving
and quit all the fuss.

To treat people fairly,
the way that we should.
And look out for others
above our own good.
To treat no one special
because of their name.
But to honor each other
for we are the same.
To lift up and carry
all who are weak.
As we grasp the importance
of living as meek.

Jesus did tell us
as He sat on a mount.
The overlooked people,
they really do count.
Instead of the fighting
as we stand up tall.
Be more like Jesus,
be a servant to all.
So when you do wonder
just where you do rate.
Take a lesson from Jesus,
it's the servant who's great!

I had a chance to relax and just spend some quiet time with God as I head into the weekend. As I did so, yet another poem appeared in my mind so I collected it to share. I pray that God uses this, and each of these poems He has given me, for His glory and for the benefit of His people and His kingdom.

Prayer Points

- Pray for the humility to understand that the "top of the heap" mentality is not in line with the priorities God desires for us to have.

- Pray that God would help you to examine the times and areas of your life when you tend to use people rather than serve them. Pray that you would repent and do what is right.

- Pray for the courage to abandon all forms of favoritism and partiality as you serve others in the name of Jesus.

- Pray for eyes that would actually see the people behind the faces of the overlooked, lonely, hungry, and needy.

- Pray that an accurate view of yourself from God's perspective would give you an accurate view of others.

- Pray that you would lift up the unappreciated as valuable in the sight of God.

- Pray that the people around you today would recognize the greatness of Jesus as you serve in His name.

Growth

Growing's not easy
to do on our own.
For growth comes about
by the seeds that are sown.
To grow in good deeds,
what do you plant?
When your mind keeps on saying,
"To do that, I can't."

"I can do all things
as He give me strength."
Does my life reflect that,
do I live at such length?
Do I seek something easy
and just what I know.
Then sit back and wonder
why my life doesn't grow.

To grow as it ought to,
a plant needs some sun.
It also needs rain
before it is done.
Our life's not that different,
The Son helps us grow.
But so does the rain,
the pain that we know.

As I was thinking about spring's eventual arrival and the beauty that arrives with spring growth, God gave me this poem. I pray that it brings glory to His name and serves the purpose for which He gave it.

In prayer,
Tom

Prayer Points

- Pray that you would always have the desire to grow in the grace of our Lord.

- Pray that you would pay close attention to the seeds that you allow to be planted in your life.

- Pray that God would help you to prioritize your time so that you would be faithful in planting the seeds of God's Word in your life.

- Pray for the courage to believe God can, and wants to, do in and through you the things that He calls for you to do.

- Pray that you would have an acceptance and understanding of how the trials of life help you to grow.

- Pray that you would pay attention to the types of seeds you are planting in the lives of others through your words, actions, and attitudes.

- Pray for the wisdom to praise God for the rain that comes into your life to cause seasons of growth and refreshing.

- Pray that you would consistently spend time with Jesus so His presence in your life can help the planted seeds of His Word to grow.

- Pray that the people around you today would give glory to God for the growth that He brings.

Helpful Words

Collecting these poems
has been quite a trip.
If I think of it much
my mind still does flip.
I even have poems
that pass through my brain.
My mind is uncertain
so to share, I refrain.
It's not that they're bad,
they all are quite true.
I think some are for me
while some are for you.

Sometimes it does seem
that many do think.
From speaking their thoughts,
they never should shrink.
If they have a thought
show up in their head.
Of course they will speak it,
it has to be said.
We live in a time
when we think it's our right.
To say what we want
no matter who is in sight.

It seems we've forgotten
an important fact.
To think first of others
is how we should act.
And part of our action
is the way we do speak.
So guard your words closely
their good you would seek.
Truth doesn't sink in
if we have no love.
And love that is pure
must come from above.

So when words do hurt,
in whole or in part.
Look so much closer,
examine the heart.
Sometimes words hurt
because we must learn.
The truth of the words
is what we did earn.
If love is the motive
that drives what we do.
The hurt isn't fatal
it's meant to help you.

This I do know
because of what I have read.
I open the Bible
and read what God said.
Some of His words
cut straight to the heart.
But His love does fill me,
so healing can start.
To be more like Jesus,
that is my aim.
So I pray that my words
would do just the same.

My mind seems to be filled with poems lately. Some specifically remind me of God's love and care through very difficult circumstances and in the midst of feelings of unjust treatment, at various times in my life. While these have brought me great peace and comfort, it seems like I get a very clear "not now" when I think about sharing them. As a couple of those were going through my head this morning, reminding me of God's goodness, He put this poem in my mind to share with you. I pray that it is a help and encouragement to you and that it brings glory to God.

Prayer Points

- Pray that God would give you the wisdom to know when to speak, but more importantly, to know when not to speak.

- Pray that you would accurately evaluate the things that you share — not only for truth, but for their usefulness in building up and encouraging rather than tearing down and destroying.

- Pray that God would filter your thoughts so that your words and actions are helpful and not hurtful.

- Pray that the people around you today would only see and hear things from you that are for their benefit and that will draw them closer to Jesus.

- Pray that you would examine the source when words hurt to see if the hurt is coming from a conviction of the Holy Spirit in your life.

- Pray that you would allow God's words of conviction to bring about a greater healing in your life rather than causing hurt.

- Pray that you would have the wisdom to accurately handle the Word of God so that your use of it brings about restoration rather than damage.

Honesty

There's something I've noticed
that really seems strange.
When it comes to truth,
we think there's a range.
There are bold lies and white lies,
and "honest to God".
And all kinds of gray space
that really seems odd.
Whatever happened
to yes and to no?
And keeping our word
wherever we go?

To keep to my word,
and make sure it's true.
Should be how I live,
when I talk with you.
I must be careful
to weigh every word.
So only the truth,
is that which is heard.
To make up a story,
so I don't look bad.
Will only bring problems,
the worst that I've had.

Image is everything,
at least we've been told.
So we make up a story
and hope that it's sold.
Our yes isn't yes,
and our no isn't no.
We consider our image
and we answer so-so.
We hide the true facts,
that we don't want seen.
And tell a new version,
where the truth is quite lean.

This doesn't mean
you should tell all you know.
Some things are private,
from your mouth should not go.
But that is a story
for another day.
About speaking the truth,
this poem will stay.
When we cover up
the truth with a lie.
Our reputation
has begun to die.

We must be careful
that we don't deceive.
By the impression
that we try to leave.
We should not have to
swear this is true.
Our word should be good
when given to you.
The things that we value
will carry more weight.
When we are honest
in all that we state.

So when you are thinking
that truth can't be found.
Open the Bible,
take a good look around.
The truth that is Jesus,
does show us the way.
And calls us to choose;
in our speech, there's no gray.
To be fully honest,
in word and in deed.
Is a teaching of Jesus
that we ought to heed.

It seems like we live in a time when so many people have lost sight of the value that God places on honesty. In the past, I've had ministry leaders tell me I'm too honest; that I should be more creative with the facts to give people an impression that was different from what was true. It also appears common to play loose with Bible texts to try to prove what we want. As I watched some of that unfold on social media, I spent time with God listening to His voice and He gave me this poem. I pray that it is an encouragement to each of us to live an honest life in our pursuit of God.

Prayer Points

- Pray that God would help you to always live in such a way that your yes is yes and your no is no.

- Pray that you would have the courage to reject the temptation to justify things that are untrue.

- Pray that your actions would always show a true belief in the things you say.

- Pray that you would have the wisdom to know when to keep silent about things you shouldn't share.

- Pray that your motives in communication would always be pure with no agenda to mislead.

- Pray that you would make every effort to keep your word, especially when it becomes difficult to do so.

The Kings

As I get ready
to teach Second Kings.
Some people do tell me
they want current things.
My answer to them
is "open the book."
Read from its pages
and take a good look.
Change a few places,
change a few names.
We're not all that different
despite all our claims.

Why do we try
so hard to avoid.
Reading of things
of which we have toyed.
Could it just be
we don't like to read.
Reminders of danger
we'd rather not heed?
We like to think,
as we see their defeat.
They made mistakes
that we'd never repeat.

Look in the mirror
and check out the news.
Pursuing God first,
we don't always choose.
His discipline comes
and we are quite shocked.
But how very often
His name, have we mocked?
We need to learn
how people did live.
To help us pursue Him
and the good He would give.

> The history God gives me,
> I should not ignore.
> He has a reason
> that He's given it for.
> He wants me to learn
> a lesson or two.
> On how I should seek Him
> and how to treat you.
> To seek Him above
> all other things.
> Is a lesson that's found
> in the books of the Kings.

I was spending time with God and going through tonight's Bible study lesson from 2 Kings and a poem started to appear. I thought it was just going to be one verse/stanza just for fun, but it kept flowing. I pray that God uses this for His glory and purposes.

Prayer Points

- Pray that God would help you to see His purpose and value in giving us the Old Testament books of the Bible as well as the New.

- Pray that your reading and study of God's Word would help you to see and avoid the pitfalls that are common to mankind.

- Pray that God's Word would teach you the purpose of His discipline that you experience.

- Pray that the people around you today would recognize the honor that you give God when you place a high value on His Word.

Life's Journey

We all have a choice
each day that we live.
Are we about taking
or all about give?
It has been said
a long time ago.
Two paths through the woods,
on which will you go?
Look back even further
the story's the same.
A wide path and narrow,
which one will you claim?

A way that seems right
in the mind of a man.
It leads to destruction
if it isn't God's plan.
We like things our way,
we think we're so smart.
If it works for the world,
how can we fall apart?
When we still struggle
with what we can't get.
It's time to look upward
before we forget.

The path that's less traveled
in this life, you see.
Is the one that serves others
instead of just me.
To start on that journey
I give up my greed.
I look out for others
to see what they need.
I look up to Jesus
to start every day.
This journey goes forward
when He leads the way.

So as you consider
the paths before you.
Which will you follow,
what will you do?
Will you follow Jesus
and the life that He led?
He cared for the people
to the point that He bled.
So in this life's journey
your choice I do pray.
Is the one beside Jesus
and that you'd never stray.

The poems just keep filling my head and if I don't type them out my mind seems to clog up. I figure since I'm typing them, I may as well share them. I pray that they serve the purpose for which God is giving them to me.

Prayer Points

- Pray that God's Spirit would help you to accurately evaluate the path you are choosing to walk through this life.

- Pray that you would recognize where the path you are on differs from the ways of God so that you can change where you are walking.

- Pray that you would see the value that others have in helping, and keeping, you on the path of God.

- Pray that the people around you today would recognize that you are walking a path that is different from the way of the world.

Listen

Like it or not
we need to find.
Inside of our head,
somewhere in our mind.
Something that's missing,
something that's rare.
To open our ears
and show that we care.
Everyone seems to
have something to say.
No one is listening,
we just go our own way.

Lazy or careless,
either could be.
I can't seem to help it
if no one hears me.
So many people
trying to be heard.
Today there's no chance
to get in a word.
Even more sad
is this little news.
No one hears God
when they do what they choose.

Listen intently
to this little poem.
In hope you'll be ready
when it's time to go home.
Search deep within you
for what you must do.
To listen to Jesus
when He calls for you.
Eagerly seek Him
with all that you are.
Notice He's waiting,
He's close and not far.

Here's another poem for what it is worth. Once the idea of it sparks in my mind, the poem falls out of my head so quickly that it is often hard to keep up. I pray that God helps us to listen more intently to each other, and especially to Him!

Prayer Points

- Pray that God would help you to actually hear what people are saying, and even what they are not saying.

- Pray that your listening to them will help people see a God that cares about them.

- Pray for the patience to wait when it is tempting to speak up and dominate a conversation.

- Pray that your continual practice of listening to God would prepare you to better listen to people.

- Pray that your obedience to the Word of God would show to the people around you just how much value you place on listening to Him.

- Pray that the people around you today will know you as one who will listen to them in a manner that shows a genuine care and concern.

- Pray that you would always be more concerned about God's Word being heard than about you being heard.

- Pray that you would be quick to listen, slow to speak, and slow to become angry.

Listening Times

The temp was at zero
as far as I know.
But the wind, it was blowing,
felt like twenty below.
I bundled in layers
to clear off the walk.
And as I was shoveling
I let God's Spirit talk.
There were no distractions,
no one else was there.
It was great God and me time
and I felt His great care.

There's times we don't feel like
the things we must do.
At least that is me,
I don't know about you.
In all of those moments
I do have a choice.
I can spend the time grumbling
or hearing God's voice.
The day goes much better
if I stop to hear.
God's calming message
that He is always near.

I pray that you listen
to the words of this poem.
That you listen to God
both at work and at home.
And as you are hearing
what God wants to say.
All things are different
when God leads the way.
So whatever you're doing,
whether happy or not.
Let God walk right with you
He's there on the spot!

While it was bitterly cold as I cleared walks this morning, it was a good listening time as I opened my heart and mind to God. In doing so, He put this poem in my mind so I could share it when I came in . . . now to find that hot tub. I pray that you continually grow in listening to God in any and all circumstances.

Prayer Points

- Pray that God would help you to understand His continual presence so the idea of ceaseless prayer would be a reality.

- Pray that God would guard your attitude as you go about routine and menial tasks.

- Pray that you would reject the temptation to grumble by using those times to actively listen to the voice of God in prayer.

- Pray that God would use your good attitude to cause people to ask about the hope that you express.

- Pray that you would always see Christ as your Lord and be ready to give gentle and respectful answers to all who would wonder about the difference your relationship with Jesus makes.

- Pray that the people around you today would see the joy of the Lord through you because of the time you spend in prayer listening to Him.

Living Hope

I turn on the news
and what do I see?
People are dying,
even people like me.
We want to feel safe
wherever we are.
But we're often in danger
even in our own car.
We think for a moment,
but not for too long.
Would I be a hero,
would I be that strong?

We're looking for answers
on how this all stops.
Perhaps if Big Brother
would provide us more cops.
If we made it much harder
for men to be armed.
Do you really think that
we couldn't be harmed?
For there's always that someone
who will still find a gun.
They'll go out and shoot you
'cause they think it is fun.

Before you're too worried
that hope can't be found.
Go pick up a Bible,
take a good look around.
On all of these pages
that God chose to give.
Are words that should help us
know just how to live.
Words that bring comfort,
words that are true.
Words that when shared
can bring hope to you, too.

In the midst of such heartache,
in the midst of such loss.
These words point to Jesus
as he hung on a cross.
"Father, forgive them"
were the words that He prayed.
His heart had compassion
on those who had strayed.
Before we look outward,
we must look within.
Father, come cleanse me
and forgive all my sin.

It's only when we take
God's Word as the norm.
That we have a message
with power to transform.
I pray that you're living
a life that is free.
So as people do watch you,
it's Jesus they see.
And as you encounter
a world that's a mess.
You share with them Jesus,
who so wants to bless.

I've been using the local news as a prayer guide this morning and this poem appeared in my mind as a result. I pray that God continues to equip and encourage His people to be the light of the world wherever they are so that the world will see the true Living Hope.

In prayer,
Tom

Prayer Points

- Pray that God would help you to remember to use your various news sources as prayer guides each day.

- Pray that your recognition of the frailty of life would motivate you to be more bold about sharing the message of the good news of Jesus.

- Pray that those who are involved in violence would experience a change of heart through a relationship with Jesus.

- Pray that you would be equipped through your relationship with Jesus to share the good news that is found in the Word of God with people who are impacted by senseless tragedy.

- Pray that you would experience the freedom of forgiveness that Jesus offers at such a level that it compels you to forgive others.

- Pray that the people around you today would see and recognize the light of Jesus shining through you regardless of the day's circumstances.

- Pray that you would take the lessons you have learned from the hard times of life and use them to extend comfort and compassion to people who are in the midst of hard times with little hope.

- Pray that at every opportunity, you would extend the true hope that is only found in Jesus.

Mirror, Mirror

I look in the mirror
and what do I see?
Do I even like
the person staring at me?
Sometimes it's easy
without looking too far.
To measure my worth
by the depth of my scar.
The true value's hidden
and hard to appear.
When I view who I am
by the things I do hear.

You're lazy, you're stupid,
you don't do enough.
When compared to all others
you don't have the right stuff.
You don't belong here,
you're really quite weird.
As a matter of fact,
I can't stand your gray beard.
The list could keep going
with many more things.
If I listen too closely,
in my ears it all rings.

Sometimes it's harder,
I'm sorry to say.
To look at things different
and see a new way.
Instead of opinions
that others do tell.
I fix my thoughts heavenward,
on Christ they do dwell.
He gives a new image
of what I should see.
When the face in the mirror
looks right back at me.

> He sees a new person,
> a child that belongs.
> All of the labels
> washed away with the wrongs.
> He gives me a new name
> and a robe that is white.
> He calls me to follow
> as He makes everything right.
> I've learned to trust Him
> when in the mirror I gaze.
> Everything's clearer
> when it's Jesus I praise!

I was eating lunch in my office and praying for a family who was in the building for a memorial service and this poem just rolled out of my mind. I don't know that it was related to the memorial service at all, but perhaps in this quiet time with God it came from recent reminders of inadequacies and failures others have labeled me with. I pray that it is an encouragement and comfort to someone and brings glory to God!

Prayer Points

- Pray that you would always recognize the value that you have in the eyes of God regardless of what people think or say.

- Pray that God would use you to express to others the value that they have in His sight.

- Pray that the people around you today would be able to see themselves as God sees them and praise Him for His great love.

My Part

To read through the Bible,
there are many claims.
Of people who started,
then they hit all those names.
From person to person
and who begat who.
The mind starts to numb
and then we are through.
We put down the Bible
and our reading does stop.
Our intended effort
becomes a great flop.

As I am preaching
through the book of Luke.
I come to these names
and I'd rather not puke.
So I look more closely
at what's written there.
And see in this listing,
a God who does care.
He lists all these people
and calls them by name.
They were important,
though most had no fame.

We have great value
as woman and man.
For we have a part in
God's wonderful plan.
God uses people
like you and like me.
To accomplish His purpose
throughout history.
He doesn't measure
like most people do.
You have great potential
when He lives in you.

If God could use people
that nobody knew.
And use them so greatly,
then He can use you.
One of the secrets
of living this way.
Is pursuing God fully,
hearing what He would say.
Then take His full message,
with others do share.
Then show them that Jesus
and you really care.

It is in this caring,
that people will see.
God's love is for them,
not only for me.
My part may seem little,
not important at all.
But that doesn't mean
the result will be small.
I will never know,
unless a list I receive.
Just how many names
did help me to believe.

So, what is your story?
What will your legacy be?
How many people,
will you help to see?
Will you be faithful,
in doing your part?
That helps someone out there,
to open their heart.
You may get no credit,
even if you should.
The real joy comes later,
when He says, "faithful and good".

I am spending time with God, going over the end of Luke chapter 3, as He refines the sermon I'll share tonight. As I am doing so, He put this poem in my mind for me to share. I pray that it brings glory to His name and accomplishes His purposes for it.

Prayer Points

- Pray that God would help you to understand His purpose for all of His Word.

- Pray for a greater understanding of the purpose of "ordinary" people in the Bible.

- Pray that what you learn from a study of God's Word will help you to see the value that God has created in each person.

- Pray that you would always find satisfaction in being faithful to what God has created you to be.

- Pray that God would help you to see more clearly how to use His gifting in your life to serve others.

- Pray that you would not give in to the temptation of fame being more important than faithfulness.

- Pray for a healthy pride in being the part of the body of Christ that God has created you to be.

- Pray for opportunities to share your story of God working in and through you.

New Man

I went to bed early
to get some good rest.
It seems I need more sleep
so that I do my best.
So I sleep for eight hours,
even more if I can.
And while it does help,
I don't wake a new man.
Perhaps it is needed
as I fight this cold.
Though some actually say,
it's because I am old.

We go to extremes
to change who we are.
We exercise more,
even buy a new car.
We spend so much time
on the way that we look.
That we fail to reflect
what is in the Good Book.
Somehow we think
if we change the outside.
No one will care much
about what is inside.

If I really want,
a new man to be.
I will change what I want,
and how I do see.
I will look on the inside,
more than what's out.
For the battle within
can be quite a bout.
Take every thought captive,
don't give it a place.
To take root and grow,
then spew out of my face.

To be the new man,
that God wants of me.
I rest in the Lord,
His face I do see.
When I become weary
and feeling quite weak.
I wait on the Lord
and His presence I seek.
The times of refreshing
in sickness and health.
Is a joy for the ages,
even more than great wealth.

When I'm under the weather,
or feeling my age.
God's Spirit is with me
and helps me engage.
A body that's rested
and a mind that is fresh.
Helps me listen to God
as His Word and I mesh.
It is not the sleep
that's important to me.
But the new man in Christ
that I want to be.

I've been feeling tired and going to bed early to get more rest so I'm ready to start an early day of building prep and cleaning. This poem began to form in my mind last night before I fell asleep and God finished it up as I did my morning work. I pray that it encourages you in your efforts to be the person that God has called you to be.

In prayer,
Tom

Prayer Points

- Pray that God would help you to understand the new creation He has made you to be.

- Pray that any attempts to improve yourself would always include a time of seeking what God wants you to be.

- Pray that deliberate time in God's Word would always be central to your plans to improve.

- Pray that you would always allow God's Spirit to work in your life as you take every thought captive.

- Pray that God would transform your thought life to make it completely pure and holy.

- Pray that you would learn to willingly wait upon the Lord to allow His renewing of your life to take place.

- Pray that you would recognize that your need for rest is by God's design.

- Pray that your life would always reflect to the people around you the new person that God has made you to be in Christ Jesus.

- Pray that your time with God would always make you feel like the new person that you are.

- Pray that the people around you today would not only see, but hear from you how God has made you new.

New Year's Opportunity

As the days slip away
and the new year does come,
Look back for a moment
and see what you've done.
Don't look for too long
or you'll fail to see,
Good things are coming
and great things will be.
The hard times aren't over
for they help us grow.
So trusting in Jesus
is the only way to go!

So, what will the year bring?
I'll just wait and see.
I'll be looking and watching
while on bended knee.
While my view is clouded,
there's One who does know.
What I will be doing
and where will I go.
There's only one answer
that will get us through.
It's to follow the Savior
as He makes us new.

So, don't you be worried
and don't you go fret.
God's work within us
is not over yet.
We'll take the good times
along with the bad.
And trust that our Father
will soon make us glad.
And as we're rejoicing
at what He has done.
We'll be looking toward heaven
and life with the Son!

I pray that these words are an encouragement to you. It continues to amaze me that these are not only in my head, but they somehow come out. May God lead and guide you throughout the new year!

Prayer Points

- Pray that God would give you a clear mind to see how He has worked in your life over the past year.

- Pray that you would find the balance of learning from the past without dwelling on it.

- Pray that you would faithfully seek God for His direction for the future.

- Pray that God's Spirit would fill you with an incredible trust as He calls you to walk each day by faith.

- Pray that you would be an encouragement to the people in your life who seem to be trapped by things of their past, good or bad, that they can't seem to let go of.

- Pray that you would understand the view that we each have is rather cloudy compared to the view that God has.

- Pray that you would grow from the hard times that God brings you through and that you will use that growth to help others turn to Jesus in the midst of difficult times.

Opinions

We all have opinions
that we hold to as fact.
They are often seen
in the way that we act.
We stand up and shout
in a voice that is loud.
I simply know more,
it's not that I'm proud.
We see this in others
throughout the whole day.
But to see it in my life,
there's simply no way.

It seems far too often,
and without any proof.
We repeat what we hear
from the top of the roof.
We hear what we like
and we make up our mind.
We're so very certain,
that the truth we don't find.
We think we're important
if we know it all.
So we fail to notice
that we're bound for a fall.

We live in a time
when it's easy to do.
To let people know
just what is our view.
I see it on-line,
in response to all news.
They're only right
if they do what I choose.
It is quite amazing
what people believe.
There's no rhyme or reason,
to the comments they leave.

If things are done one way,
it's completely wrong.
But do them the other,
they sing the same song.
You can't win for losing,
is what some will say.
But I choose to believe
there's a much better way.
I need to be careful
before I reply.
Before I do answer,
I ought to ask, "Why?".

Not only ask why,
but ask what is true.
That my answer is godly,
not just my own view.
To consider the matter
beyond what is shown.
And try to see clearly,
as if their shoes were my own.
What I think doesn't matter,
if it's really off-base.
And I only know that,
when I seek my God's face.

So when I read something
of which I don't agree.
I look to God's Word
to see if it's me.
When there is a difference
of opinion, not fact.
I guard my words closely
and watch how I act.
I choose to know one thing
and it's always true.
It's more than opinion,
that God does love you.

Social media seems to make it easy for people to express their opinions with little regard for truth, fact, or even the whole story. As I was reflecting this morning on comments I have read about various postings and news items, God put this poem in my mind. I pray that it helps you to consider the words you use and examine the difference between opinion and truth before you feel obligated to comment.

Prayer Points

- Pray that you would always express the difference between opinion and fact in your speech.

- Pray that you would be filled with a humility that allows for others to have an opinion that is different from yours.

- Pray that God's Word would always be the source for your opinions, as well as for what you present as fact.

- Pray that God would fill you with a wisdom that would protect you from giving foolish answers that are grounded solely in opinion.

- Pray that you would have the patience to listen to what a person is actually saying before you respond.

- Pray that you would not give in to peer pressure and accept the opinions of people as fact just because they are popular.

Origins

I hear that last night
there was a debate.
Did things simply happen
or did God create.
I did not watch it
nor listen at all.
So who was the winner,
you make the call.
Someone more studied
and smarter than I.
Watched the whole thing
and said it was a tie.

Faith can be difficult
and hard to explain.
I believe the Bible
so some think I'm insane.
To prove my existence
is easy you see.
But how I am formed
is a great mystery.
We study and learn,
we map DNA.
But where did it come from,
many people won't say.

To bring order from chaos
is quite a big change.
To say it just happened,
to me seems quite strange.
We want more answers
than what we have got.
To figure it all out,
we simply will not.
For me it is easy
to trust what God does.
I don't spend time thinking
of exactly what was.

Say I am ignorant,
if that's what you must.
There is nothing you say
that will destroy my trust.
God lives within me,
His Spirit I feel.
I see Him work through me,
I know He is real.
I don't have the answers
you may want to hear.
But I trust my creator
and I know He is near.

So how do I live
in the midst of debate?
To convince you I'm right
doesn't decide my fate.
And while I am thankful
for those who explain.
To argue and fight,
we must fully refrain.
To be an example,
that Christ I would show.
To help those around me,
His mystery to know.

I have read throughout the day various comments about the creation/evolution debate that took place last night. As I was spending time with God this afternoon, He put this poem in my mind for me to collect and share. This is not a commentary on the debate itself as I did not watch or listen to any of it. Rather, I think it has more to do with our desire to have all the answers and to always be right — sometimes we don't like to leave room for "the great mystery". I pray that this poem brings glory to God and accomplishes His purpose for it.

Prayer Points

- Pray that you would not get caught up in foolish arguments with people who have no desire for anything but conflict.

- Pray that you would recognize when God has softened a heart and prepared it to listen to truth.

- Pray that you would always be prepared to give an answer for the hope that you have.

- Pray that your faith would be strengthened through the mystery of creation and mankind's existence.

- Pray that the scientists who study mankind and creation would be overwhelmed with the evidence of a creator and that there would be people in their life to introduce them to the God who created everything.

- Pray that your defense of creation would honor God and that your emotions would not take you beyond what God has revealed.

- Pray that you would live at peace with those who come to different conclusions than you do about creation in areas that God has not specifically revealed to us in His Word.

- Pray that you would always celebrate the unfathomable depths of God's knowledge which are beyond all of mankind's efforts of understanding.

Others

The way we treat others
will say quite a lot.
Not really about them,
more about what we've got.
Do I have compassion
and kindness for those.
That God puts around me,
not just those I chose.
Do I tend to order
and boss those around.
Who don't benefit me,
at least that I've found.

It would be quite funny,
if it wasn't so sad.
There have been leaders
who have treated me bad.
But that's not important
in what I will do.
The much bigger issue
is how I treat you.
Do I look beyond all
the things people see.
And love you like Jesus
has shown love to me.

It is so easy
to love those like us.
And think that those different
are not worth the fuss.
It can take much effort
to see in the heart.
But we'll never get there
if we refuse to start.
It can be quite risky
to let down our guard.
But Jesus did warn us
to follow Him would be hard.

When we show great favor
to those who repay.
We've not lived like Jesus,
at least that's what He'd say.
To give to the needy
what they can't return.
Is a lesson from Jesus
that we all need to learn.
To lift up the weak
and carry their load.
Is a way to serve others
as we all walk this road.

So what will you do
with the choices you make?
When you deal with people
will you give, not just take?
Will you listen closely
to all that you hear?
And pay close attention
to what's hidden by fear.
To treat people better
than others might do.
To give them the treatment
that you'd want for you.

When you stop and think
of what Jesus taught.
To go and do likewise,
then really you ought.
There's no better time
to begin in that way.
To do good to others
by starting today.
And when I say "others",
I mean everyone.
To put into practice
what we've learned from the Son.

God gave me this poem last night as I spent time with Him in prayer and listening. This time I jotted it down so I wouldn't forget it when I finally made it to the computer. I pray that it encourages each of us to see others as God sees them.

Prayer Points

- Pray that God would help you to clearly see the way in which you treat others.

- Pray that God's Spirit would help you examine your heart and motives to understand why you treat people the way you do.

- Pray that the way you treat people would always be a reflection of the way God treats you, not a reflection of the way people treat you.

- Pray that God would open your heart to see His view of people who are different from you.

- Pray that you would have the courage to reject favoritism and the prevalent practice of doing good only to those who can repay the favor.

- Pray that God would help you to see the others who can never repay but that He has called you to serve.

- Pray that the people around you today would experience the love of Jesus through you, regardless of who they are.

Our Mission

I have a mission
and so do you, too.
It's a mission for all
and not just a few.
There are so many
who still need to know.
Jesus commanded
to tell as we go.
To live it and teach it
and help people see.
My life has real purpose
with Jesus in me.

To always be ready
to share the Good News.
To share it with all,
not just those we choose.
But as we do share
with people each day.
Be gentle and kind
in the things we do say.
To set apart Christ,
as Lord of our life.
Treat the Word carefully,
it's as sharp as a knife.

We want to help healing
and not cause a mess.
Some times I have botched it,
of that, I confess.
God's Word can be cutting,
right down to the bone.
So we must be careful,
we don't act on our own.
God's Spirit lives in us
to help as we talk.
And sometimes He leads us
to silently walk.

To speak up or show up,
should not be our choice.
If we listen to Jesus
and obey His voice.
Sometimes He leads us
to sit for a while.
It could be a person
only needs a big smile.
When words are in order,
how careful are we?
To point to the Savior,
instead of at "me"?

We like to have answers
to show we are smart.
But it's only God's power
that can transform a heart.
So as we consider,
a commission so great.
We must be about it,
lost people can't wait.
We tell a great message
that they can receive.
God's goodness and mercy,
if they would believe.

That is our mission
that God calls us to.
To share the Good News
that can make us all new.
We tell of Jesus,
immersing in His name.
His blood does cleanse us
and removes all our shame.
We teach His commandments
as response to His love.
And He remains with us
as He reigns from above.

I was spending time with God this afternoon in preparation for tonight's Bible study I will lead from 2 Kings 7. The chapter deals with the story of some men with leprosy discovering some very good news and then having to decide what they would do with that good news. As I reflected on that story, God put this poem in my mind dealing with the Good News that we have in Jesus and the decision we must make about what we will do with it. I pray that this poem brings glory to God and accomplishes His purposes for it.

Prayer Points

- Pray that you would be faithful in fulfilling the mission that God has called you to.

- Pray that you would see each person in your life as an opportunity to share the gospel.

- Pray that you would allow God's Spirit to destroy pride in your life that keeps you from seeing people who are different from you.

- Pray that you would share the truth of God's Word in the things you do and say, but allow God to do the work of changing a person's heart.

- Pray that God would fill you with great wisdom in knowing when and how to tell your story of God's transformation in your life.

- Pray that you would have the courage to share the full message of the gospel and call people to accept the life-transforming message of Jesus.

Overcomers

It's been quite a year
as I look around.
Some dreams were lost
while others were found.
When life doesn't turn out
quite as I planned,
I still trust the Holy One
who is holding my hand.
It's my faith in Jesus
that helps me get through.
I hope and I pray
that is true for you, too.

When people mistreat you
and life seems unfair,
Look to your Savior
'cause He'll always care.
It may take much longer
than you think it should,
But God still does promise
it will be for your good.
When this life is over,
if you can recall,
All of those hardships
will seem kind of small.

So look at what matters
and see what will last.
Having such vision
can conquer the past.
The things thought important
may not really be.
If they last for a moment
instead of eternally.
So don't be too worried
what people might say.
As long as you're ready
for God's judgment day.

> When living in this world
> it's so hard to think.
> That all of my "good" stuff
> could be gone in a wink.
> So handle possessions
> with a very loose grip.
> Then it's not so painful
> when they start to slip.
> Invest all your treasure
> in what cannot be lost.
> For it has great value
> no matter the cost.

I pray that these words accomplish the purpose for which God gave them to me. Perhaps part of that purpose is for you.

Prayer Points

- Pray that your relationship with Jesus would be an encouragement to others when they experience shattered dreams.

- Pray that you would always view the disappointments of life through the wide-angle view of eternity.

- Pray that you would hold loosely to the things of this world — whether material possessions or dreams — for they are all temporary and will be given up at some point in time.

- Pray that you would be diligent about laying up your treasure in heaven by investing in sharing the gospel of Jesus with others.

Overflow

We say what we want,
thinking it's no big deal.
If we do wound others
a "sorry" will heal.
But how sorry are we
about what we said?
Or do we shift blame
to how it's taken instead?
If they would relax,
lighten up, and just chill.
I gave it no thought,
I never meant ill.

Perhaps that's the problem
that we fail to see.
We opened our mouth,
never counting to three.
The three's not important,
it's more about thought.
Do I think before speaking,
as I know I ought.
When I stop to consider,
what my words will do.
I need to quit looking
at me and see you.

Words will stay with us,
they're hard to erase.
They get in our mind and
they dig in some place.
And when least expected,
They jump right on out.
They may make us happy,
or may make us pout.
The words you are using,
just what will they mean?
When months and years later,
they're still on the scene.

You may be thinking,
I've got this all wrong.
Words don't stay with me,
at least not for long.
I can't be certain,
if that's true for you.
But based on who I know,
you'd be one of a few.
Even when I've thought
words rolled off my back.
In the right setting,
they've found their way back

There is a good side
to a mind that will store.
I praise God with songs
from when I was four.
The thing that's important,
is to guard what goes in.
So what comes out later,
doesn't cause us to sin.
When I seek Jesus
to fill my whole heart.
The words that I should say
have a great place to start.

For out of my mouth comes,
a great overflow.
Of what Jesus put in me,
and of just who I know.
The treasure inside me
can't be hidden for long.
For God's love does fill me
with a prayer and a song.
And since it's His Spirit
that I have in me.
My words should reflect that,
so it's Him people see.

I was outside this afternoon enjoying the sunshine while getting some things done around the building and found myself singing some Sunday School songs from way back in my childhood. As I considered the power words have had in my life, God gave me this poem to share. I pray that it encourages you and I to be careful with our words.

Prayer Points

- Pray that God would help you to always put a guard over your tongue.

- Pray that you would have the courage to take responsibility for the times when your words cause hurt.

- Pray that God's Spirit would help you to be quick to listen, slow to speak, and slow to become angry.

- Pray that you would understand the power of the words that you hold onto in your mind.

- Pray that you would be diligent in hiding God's Word in your heart.

- Pray that your mind would be filled with an abundance of good things from God's Word.

- Pray that the overflow of your heart would bring praise, honor, and glory to God.

- Pray that Jesus would be the treasure that God has put in your jar of clay for others to see.

Peace

My peace I leave with you,
my peace I do give.
Are words taught by Jesus
on how we should live.
This could be much easier,
I think you would see.
If all of the people
with me would agree.
That really won't happen,
of that I am sure.
So I better get busy,
for my pride find a cure.

God made us all different,
made each one unique.
To understand others
is what I must seek.
To see how God's gifted
and what He will use.
Since I'm not in charge,
it's not mine to choose.
Each one has something
that God's made their part.
I need to help them
find out how to start.

As you start looking
for what others have got.
This may sound quite easy,
I assure you it's not!
To think of them higher
than you do yourself.
But don't you go thinking
you've been put on the shelf.
Your gift has great value,
it's important to all.
So step out and use it
as you follow God's call.

God's peace will happen
when we swallow our pride.
When we work together
for we're on the same side.
This doesn't mean
that we'll always agree.
But peace will still come
when your value I see.
As I spend more time
on what God says to do.
I don't worry so much
what He says to you.

I'm not here to judge you
or over you rule.
Instead I'll encourage,
let you know we are cool.
With eyes fixed on Jesus,
more clearly I see.
Peace comes from heaven,
for you and for me.
So when our views differ
and we know we are right.
Let's pray to our Savior,
that He'll fix our sight.

And when He has straightened
the way that we view.
May peace rest upon me
and all over you.
And when this peace settles
on all that we are.
Let's take what we've learned
and spread it afar.
And as we go boldly
where no one would go.
I pray that God's peace
to others we show.

I was spending time with God reflecting on the incredible peace that He has given me within the family of Deer Run. It's a peace that comes from His Spirit, but also from the great encouragement and sense of value that I receive on a very regular basis from those that surround me. As I reflected on this, God put this poem in my mind for me to collect and share. I pray that it is an encouragement to you in the way you view others who may think and act differently than you do.

Prayer Points

- Pray that God would fill your heart and mind with the peace of Christ as you live among people who have different opinions than you.

- Pray that God would help you to see the value in how He has gifted each of us differently and how that gifting can be used within the body of Christ.

- Pray that God would put people around you that would confirm the value that you have to God.

- Pray that God would fill you with the humility to view yourself and others accurately.

- Pray for a discerning heart to know the difference between God's truth and your opinion.

- Pray that you would be at peace with people who think differently than you about matters of opinion while still holding to the truth of God's Word.

Perception

I parted some water
only last night.
It stacked up beside me,
it was quite a sight.
I walked right between it,
each side was a wall.
And I wasn't too worried
that either would fall.
Before you start thinking
that I've lost my mind.
The water was frozen,
it was the snowflake kind.

That may not seem funny,
or maybe it does.
Our mind paints a picture
of what is and what was.
And so very often,
it is hard to see.
Anything different
than I thought would be.
We've all heard some stories
that just can't be true.
At least 'til we see them
from a different view.

So when you do question
a story that's bold.
Look at it closely,
see what really was told.
When we start to listen
beyond "I am fine."
We may just discover
a valuable mine.
To understand others
is quite a great gift.
Our world would be different
if we all made this shift.

It will not be easy,
I know it is hard.
Sometimes we get burnt
and our spirit feels charred.
We don't have to agree
on every detail.
We still work together
so neither will fail.
So when your perception
fills you with much doubt.
Look from all angles
as you figure it out.

Perception's a problem
when we start to pray.
It's so very hard
to see things God's way.
We hold to His promise
He said in His Word.
But sometimes the answer
isn't quite like we heard.
When you expect one thing
and it's not what you get.
Look at it from God's view
and you should be all set.

I was spending time with God this morning and thinking about the work I did last night clearing walks. I realized that it was water that was stacked up on either side of me — just not liquid yet. This poem appeared in my mind as a look at the perceptions we have based on our understanding, often a one-sided understanding, of a person, an event, or even God. I pray that you constantly look at things from God's perspective to give clarity to your perception.

Prayer Points

- Pray that you would have the wisdom to accurately communicate according to the audience you are with.

- Pray that you would have the patience to seek out a clearer understanding of what you hear when the message seems to not make sense.

- Pray that God would give you a clear mind to be able to listen to and understand where people are coming from when they talk.

- Pray that God would help you to overcome any negative preconceived ideas about people when He gives you opportunity to share with them about Jesus.

- Pray that the people around you would be open to hearing the good news of Jesus without automatically dismissing it as irrelevant.

- Pray that God would help you to live your life in such a way that the people around you would believe the good news of Jesus is relevant to their life as well.

- Pray that God's Spirit would help you to remove selfishness and pride from your prayer life.

- Pray that you would have a greater belief that God's plans are always meant for your good, even when they don't turn out as you expect they should.

The Prize

The Olympics are here
and so we are told.
It's only the winners
who will receive gold.
The athletes have trained
and worked for so long.
To prove they're the fastest,
the best, and the strong.
But in such a group
where the best surely rise.
In each competition,
only one gets top prize.

So what can we say
about all the rest?
Who have no gold medal
though they did their best.
Someone did better
or something went wrong.
The world looks at them
as if they don't belong.
As hard as they work
and as much as they try.
Sometimes they're left sitting
and wondering why.

To the strong goes the prize,
at least that we say.
But what if they're strong
in a much different way?
To be faithful in small things,
God calls us to be.
The little things matter,
though no one may see.
The true test of strength
is what will you do,
When no one is watching
or looking at you?

You may be able
to hide from all men.
But God will still notice,
what will you do then?
To give Him your all
is all that He asks.
To put Him before
all your other tasks.
To train your mind daily
to look all around.
With all your heart seek God
and He will be found.

The prize will be given
when you finish this race.
Not because you are fastest,
rather you've sought His face.
So the training continues
as this life you live.
You reflect Jesus
when to others you give.
To give yourself fully
like God's only Son.
To finish the race
and He says, "Well done."

I spent some time with God this morning and thought about the Olympics as they began last night. God gave me this poem as a reminder that in His view, it is the faithful who win the prize. I am thankful for God's faithfulness, mercy, and grace so that a performance mistake on the world's stage doesn't disqualify me nor negate all of my training. I pray that this poem brings glory to God and accomplishes the purposes for which He gave it.

Prayer Points

- Pray that God would help you to see just what it is you are pursuing in life.

- Pray that you would not be distracted by the shiny rewards of the world as you pursue the great prize of eternal life.

- Pray that you would have confidence in the power of God to carry to completion the work that He has begun in you.

- Pray that you would understand God's desire for all people to come to repentance and obtain the prize of eternal life.

- Pray for the wisdom to help others who feel they are losing out in their life pursuits.

- Pray that you would accurately evaluate, according to God's perspective, the importance of the things in your life.

- Pray that you would recognize the cost, and value, of the prize you seek.

- Pray that you would learn to give up everything to obtain the prize of the greatest value.

- Pray that you would continue to grow in faith as you engage in spiritual training.

- Pray that your life would be lived in a way that shows the people around you how to be prepared for eternity.

Practice

Advice From a Doctor
is the title I give.
To a series of sermons
on how we should live.
We'll spend a whole year,
perhaps even more.
Listening to Luke
for what he has in store.
And while we will learn
of the Christ who can save.
We'll focus more closely
on the advice that Luke gave.

So very often
when we look at God's Word.
We go out and live
like none of it was heard.
I want to do more
than know what Christ did.
I want people to see,
in my heart His Word's hid.
If sin's crucified,
as His Word does say.
Then it's not I who lives,
but He lives today.

If I have died
and He lives in me.
Then people should notice
it's Jesus they see.
So I study harder
and take a good look.
At just what He says
when I open His Book.
Not so I know it
as a collection of fact.
But that it transforms me
in the way that I act.

Jesus did tell me
to do my good deeds.
So people do see Him
as I'm meeting their needs.
To offer forgiveness
and grace without end.
To pray that they'll know Him
as redeemer and friend.
When I'm more like Jesus
to the people I meet.
Perhaps they will seek Him
and fall at His feet.

That is the purpose
of the sermons I preach.
To help us live different,
the Bible I teach.
Not so we know more
for information.
We practice it daily
for transformation.
When our life is changed
by advice that Luke gives.
We're more likely heard
when we say that Christ lives.

I've been spending time with God in the gospel of Luke as I continue preparing a sermon series that I am preaching. The point of the series is not to simply know the life of Christ for information, but to allow His life to transform the way we live. I pray that we represent Christ well in all of our interactions with people.

In prayer,
Tom

Prayer Points

- Pray that you would learn more about Christ for the purpose of living more like Christ.

- Pray that your time in God's Word would be transformational rather than just informational.

- Pray that you would learn to see people in the way that Jesus saw, and sees, them.

- Pray that you would have a greater understanding of what it means to be crucified with Christ so that you no longer live but He lives in you.

- Pray that you would be diligent about doing the good works that He has prepared in advance for you to do.

- Pray that the way in which you do your good deeds would be such that people who see them would glorify God.

- Pray that you would live your life in a way that people actually see the message that you speak.

- Pray that the Word of God becomes the foundation on which your life is built.

- Pray that the people around you today would see in you a unity and love that represents Jesus.

- Pray that God's Spirit would help you listen more purposefully every time God's Word is shared.

Pure Religion

The world is all grumpy
and people act mean.
It's all about "my rights",
or so it would seem.
We look at each other,
instead of within.
Yes, I have a problem,
it's caused by my sin.

God gives us an answer,
I believe this is true.
He sent us a Savior
to make me brand new.
When I live for Jesus,
He calls me to care,
for widows and orphans
and people out there.

To examine my own self
to see what is wrong.
Then allow Him to change it
while I praise Him in song.
My faith is not visible
by what I might say,
so I must act different
and reject my own way!

This little writing
is really quite plain,
I live for Jesus
and He keeps me sane.
The life that He gives me,
I pray for you.
That the glory of Jesus
is all that shines through!

I pray that you find some joy and encouragement through these words. I've been preaching a sermon series through the book of James and as I spent time preparing to wrap up that series, these lines just flowed from my mind. I figure that God put them there and He brought them out, so He has a purpose to use them in someone's life. I pray that someone is you!

Prayer Points

- Pray that you would respond positively to God's call to give up everything, even your rights, and follow Him.

- Pray that you would recognize the sin of selfishness and greed when it appears in your life and that you would look to the power of Jesus to remove with it.

- Pray that your pure life in Christ would motivate you to doing what He says in regard to caring for the helpless and overlooked that live in your community.

- Pray that you would daily spend time with God, allowing His Spirit to examine you and cleanse you from all the impurity of the world.

- Pray that the people around you today would see the glory of God reflected in your life through the help that you give to others and through a life of obedient purity.

Refueling

The fuel gauge said empty,
so I stopped for a fill.
It wasn't too bad
until I got the bill.
Twenty-eight gallons
in a twenty-seven tank.
It's a good thing that I
had stopped by the bank.
Running on fumes,
I did seem to be.
But was it my truck,
or was it just me?

The same thing did happen,
in my floor machine.
It ran out of power
before I could clean.
In search of an answer,
I started to read.
And found that the batteries,
some water did need.
And into each cell,
some water did pour.
I used up a gallon
and still needed more.

So very often,
as we live this life.
Our power is drained
by worry and strife.
We barely get by,
on a life out of gas.
Or we fail to function,
and just take a pass.
The answer is easier
said than it's done.
Refuel your spirit,
by time with the Son.

So when I am weary
and feeling run down.
I take off my mask
and He sees my frown.
We spend time together,
He restoreth my soul.
He fills up my tank
and makes my batteries whole.
But I've learned a lesson,
there's not so much pain.
If I refill sooner,
while some fuel does remain.

A life lived with Jesus
throughout every day.
Keeps me from empty,
as I live His way.
So instead of waiting
until I have run dry.
I hold fast to Jesus
and together we fly.
So stop what you're doing
and refill your tanks.
Give praise to the Father,
and to Jesus give thanks!

The floor scrubber at work kept running for shorter and shorter amounts of time before needing recharged. I did some research and discovered that the batteries in it are not maintenance-free and they were in desperate need of water. This reminded me of times that I have put more fuel in my truck than what the official capacity is because I had run it so close to empty. Then that reminded me of times that I have allowed my spirit to be drained due to not spending the time with God that I ought. I pray that this poem encourages you to constantly refuel your spirit with the presence of God.

Prayer Points

- Pray for those who are physically, emotionally, and/or spiritually running on empty.

- Pray that you would notice the warning signs that God gives you when you are nearing a state of emptiness.

- Pray that you would regularly set aside times of rest for all areas of your life.

- Pray that you would not allow distractions to keep you from spending regular time with God in prayer and study/reading of His Word.

- Pray that you would seek out times of refreshing even before you reach the point of exhaustion.

- Pray that you would experience God's promise of a restored soul as you walk with Him.

- Pray that you would be an instrument of God in delivering a refueling from Him to those around you in need.

- Pray for a spirit of refreshing and refueling to spread throughout your family and the entire body of Christ.

- Pray for wisdom in making the most of the refueling God gives you in order to worship Him and serve others.

- Pray for the endurance to persevere and draw on the strength of God in times when you feel drained.

Rest

We work hard, we play hard;
but what about rest.
God says we need it
to be at our best.
Our life gets so busy
at work and at play.
Our rest gets put off
for at least one more day.
So many people
work just to survive.
We don't get the rest
that would help us to thrive.

Go here and do this,
and what about that?
If you think you are done;
well, here's one more hat.
Some tasks are given,
we think there's no choice.
Others we call for
in the loudest of voice.
We need this, we want that;
we can't fall behind.
To have all that we want
takes the top of our mind.

If I don't keep going,
refusing to stop.
Then somebody else
will climb to the top.
And as I am climbing,
and taking each rod.
The ladder of this world
takes me further from God.
The king of the mountain,
the top of the hill.
Is not that important
when God says, "Be still."

Strength for the weary
and hope for the tired.
Seems so out of reach,
when you fear you'll be fired.
So onward we press
and give it our all.
We will never give up
'til we can't help but fall.
So many people
who fall flat on their face.
Need a good chance to rest
and experience grace.

So when you are tired,
it seems with no end.
Examine your schedule,
rest may be your friend.
And as you rest fully,
as God said you should.
Look for the weary
and do them some good.
Help carry their burden
and show them the need.
God's command to get rest,
they really should heed.

It has been what some would call a "lazy day", but I prefer to think of it as a "restful day". As I was resting, falling in and out of sleep, God put this poem in my mind. I am thankful for a work environment that tries to protect my need for rest by valuing the work that I do. I pray that this poem encourages you to rest and to do what you can to help others to rest.

In prayer,
Tom

Prayer Points

- Pray that God would help you to see more clearly the importance that He places on rest.

- Pray that you would understand the difference between recreation and rest, and the value that each of them have.

- Pray that God would help you to have a greater understanding of the rest that is needed by the people around you.

- Pray that you would live life in balance and value the things of God over the things of the world.

- Pray that God would help you to know the plans He has to provide for all of your needs, including your need for rest.

- Pray that God's Spirit would help you to examine how you spend your time and reveal to you any areas that are out of balance.

- Pray that God will help you to find times of rest when it feels like the demands of people make rest an elusive thing.

- Pray that you would extend grace to people who need rest.

- Pray that the people around you today would see in you the value of a life lived fully resting in Jesus.

Revival

The days of revival
have long been around.
But even with all that,
can the faithful be found?
A message of judgment
we'd rather not hear.
Tell us the good news
and leave out the fear.
But good news is lacking
if we don't tell the bad.
Our rescue from dying,
is what makes us glad.

For if there's no judgment,
when Christ I reject.
Then there is no reason,
my life to inspect.
The good news of Jesus,
calls me to believe.
The wages of my sin,
I don't have to receive.
And while it's a free gift,
it is up to me.
For I must accept it
if I want to be free.

John was sent early
to prepare the way.
To call for repentance,
and do it today.
While some liked the idea
of escaping God's wrath.
They were quite startled,
they were on the wrong path.
Some came to see him,
thinking that they were good.
They had to look closer
and then do what they should.

The one who had plenty
was to share what he had.
Those collecting taxes
should not treat people bad.
The ones with position
should not falsely accuse.
Be content with their pay,
not spreading bad news.
With someone like John
teaching that which was right.
The people suspected
that the Christ was in sight.

John quickly answered,
"The Messiah, I'm not."
But the One that is coming
has more power than I've got.
He is much greater
than one such as I.
The thongs of His sandals,
I'm not fit to untie.
He will immerse you
in His Spirit and fire.
For that which is impure,
the consequence is dire.

So what will we do
with the message we hear?
Will we praise God with joy
or tremble in fear?
The choice seems so simple,
at least it should be.
When my heart is repentant,
He will forgive me.
And when I'm forgiven,
by faith I should live.
The good news of Jesus,
to all I must give.

I've been spending time with God this afternoon in the beginning of Luke 3 as I prepare for tonight's sermon. As I was listening to God for refinement of the sermon, He put this poem in my mind. I pray that it encourages and challenges you and that it brings glory to His name.

Prayer Points

- Pray that you would see clearly any drifting you may have done that would call for a revival in your relationship with God.

- Pray that you would have a greater understanding of just how lost you would be outside of a relationship with Jesus.

- Pray for a greater realization of the incredible power of God's mercy and grace.

- Pray that your desire to escape the wrath of God would lead to a repentance from sin.

- Pray that a revival of God's Spirit in your life would produce good fruit for His kingdom.

- Pray that you would examine not only what God has provided in your life, but what He wants you to do with it.

- Pray for a life that not only proclaims Jesus, but points people to Him as the source of revival in your life and theirs.

- Pray for the wisdom and courage to call people to a revival in their life.

Snow Days

The snow just kept falling
and the temperature got cold.
All commerce did stop
and staying home got quite old.
The city shut down
like I've never seen.
When the temps bottomed out
around minus eighteen.
And on the third day
there was finally some sun.
And the temperature rose
to a warm minus one!

In the midst of such warmth
outside I must go.
I start up the blower,
the one made for snow.
I head down the drive
to clear it all out.
My world turns all white
as snow flies from the spout.
In the midst of such beauty
the cold settles in.
All the way from my toes
to the end of my chin.

My clothes are all covered
and my hat frosty white.
Now it's time to go in
so the frost doesn't bite.
As I look out the window
I like what was done.
If it wasn't so cold
it might have been fun.
Tonight I will sleep for
tomorrow's a new day.
It's supposed to be warmer
so it's work and not play.

This poem came tumbling out of my head as I was running the snow blower following several days of heavy snow and extremely cold temperatures. This one seemed to be more of a "just for fun" poem than the others, but God is free to use it however He chooses.

Prayer Points

- Pray for a heart and mind that remembers to look out for people who are living as shut-ins because of weather, or because of difficulty in getting around due to health or other issues.

- Pray for wisdom and safety for you and others in all of your activities.

- Pray that God's Spirit would remind you of His presence through the beauty of creation each day.

- Pray with thankfulness for whatever warmth and protection that God provides for you.

- Pray for the people in your community who have no place to go and must endure the harsh conditions of nature.

- Pray that God would open your eyes and heart to ways to help people who need food, clothing, and shelter.

- Pray that you would eagerly share the good news of Jesus with all who are "out in the cold".

Snowed In

It's past ten this morning
and I'm feeling fine.
The temperature outside
is a cool minus nine!
So what do I do
when the weather's so cold?
Play video games
and pretend I'm not old.
But even much better
than winning a game.
Is to spend time with God,
that's the best — I do claim!

To just read my Bible
and take time to pray.
To hear God's Holy Spirit,
He has something to say.
To listen intently
to what I should do.
Then make sure I do it,
for it might be for you.
So if you're snowed in,
with no where to be.
Try seeking God's face
while on bended knee.

If you do seek Him,
He says He'll be found.
He'll walk right there with you
as your feet hit the ground.
And when you're uncertain
of which way to go.
Ask Him to guide you,
His way you would know.
He'll never leave you
nor forsake you, it's true.
It's been true in my life,
I believe it for you.

This just popped into my mind as I was sitting at my desk going back and forth between a couple of Word's With Friends games and praying about some lessons I'm working on. I pray that you are encouraged to seek God more deliberately, and that you actually do it.

Prayer Points

- Pray that God would help you to make the most of your "free" time — finding the proper balance of rest, recreation, and spending time with Him.

- Pray that you would have the courage to remove all distractions from your life that keep you from spending the time in God's Word that you ought.

- Pray for a discerning spirit to know the voice of God and to understand what He wants you to do, then pray for the courage to do it.

- Pray that your life would speak volumes to others about a God who promises to be found when He is sought with a whole heart.

- Pray that you would seek, and listen to, God's direction for every aspect of your life.

- Pray that the people around you today would see God's presence alive and at work in your life and that He would give you opportunity to share the message of salvation with them.

The Source

From where does it come
and where does it go?
While I have an idea,
I don't really know.
I sit all alone
and open my heart.
That just seems to be
how it often will start.
But I'm not alone
as I sit before God.
He guides and directs me
with His staff and His rod.

He gives me His promise
that He will be here.
I just need to trust Him
and live with no fear.
This life won't be easy,
of this I am sure.
He told me Himself,
in His Word that is pure.
Troubles will come
and hard times will be.
I won't be alone,
I have His Spirit in me.

These poems I do write
are like the Spirit God gives.
While I don't know His path,
I am sure that He lives.
I feel Him within me,
I feel Him without.
He gives me assurance
that I don't need to doubt.
Just like the wind
that goes to and fro.
God's Spirit is with me
wherever I go.

So when you do worry
and when you do fret.
God's Spirit can calm you
when before Him you set.
You may just not notice
quite how He got here.
But His presence can fill you
so you know He is near.
And when He is in you,
this is my claim.
He will change you forever,
you'll never be the same!

I am asked often about where these poems have all of a sudden come from and it is a difficult question to answer with certainty. As I reflected on that question, a sermon I shared this morning, and thought through what God would have me share tonight, this poem filled my mind. I believe the source of these poems is God's Spirit in me and just like the unseen nature of the Spirit, there is an element of faith woven through the midst of each poem God gives me. I pray that He uses these for His glory and His purpose.

Prayer Points

- Pray that you would be open to accepting the mystery of God's working in your life.

- Pray that the people around you today would see evidence of the Holy Spirit working in you.

- Pray that you would always keep alive and share the mystery of the gospel.

Spring Thaw

The ground is all frozen
as hard as can be.
It does look all barren
if today's all you see.
The air is so cold,
it seems nothing could grow.
But the ground's just asleep
beneath a blanket of snow.
So look well beneath
the ground frozen white.
And you will soon see
everything is still right.

The rays of the sun
that will come out real soon.
Will make everything different
at least by mid-June!
The seeds that are hidden
In the ground down below.
Will be warmed by the sun
and they'll soon start to grow.
Their journey upward
may be filled with much strife.
But that's okay now
as they burst forth with life.

There's more to this story
than just the outside.
It's more about people
and what they do hide.
So very often,
at least that we're told.
People seem so hard
and their heart seems so cold.
Before you point fingers
you might look and see.
Instead of just others,
it's you and it's me.

And just like the ground
needs the sun to appear.
Our heart starts to thaw
when the Son does come near.
The warmth of God's Spirit
makes His fruit start to sprout.
And as it continues
the good deeds come out.
So look to the Savior
and see what I saw.
A life spent with Jesus
can make any heart thaw!

As I was working in the office today and noticing the steady stream of water dripping past my window from the melting snow, this poem appeared in my head. I pray that it ministers to those that God designed for it to reach.

Prayer Points

- Pray that God would help you to see beyond the frozen surface of people's lives and to see the potential that He has placed within them.

- Pray that you would consistently share the warmth of God's love with people and allow Him to cause the seed of the gospel to grow.

- Pray for a great harvest of righteousness to take place that would begin with God using a total transformation of your life to show the world that the love of Jesus can thaw the coldest of hearts.

The Story

There is a true story
that I have been told.
I do love to hear it,
it never gets old.
It's the story of Jesus
and of His great love.
How He came to earth,
descending from above.
He had a purpose
and followed a plan.
His love came to save us
as He became man.

Love was not created,
it always has been.
From the very beginning,
God knew we could sin.
But even with this fact,
He gave us His breath.
Then gave man instructions
so he could avoid death.
Satan did tempt Eve
to eat from the tree.
She called out to Adam,
"Come, eat with me."

When they had eaten,
the fruit on that day.
Their eyes became opened,
they did disobey.
God came and asked them,
"Just what have you done?"
I can almost hear them,
"We were just having fun."
But fun times were over,
at least like they'd had.
It did not take long
for life to be sad.

Life was not easy,
because of their sin.
God said He would solve it,
they didn't know when.
Many years later,
at just the right time.
God sent us a Savior,
the story's sublime!
Born in a stable,
was God's only Son.
The wise men acknowledged
that He was the One.

He lived His life perfect
and sinless and pure.
He always kept focused
on what He must endure.
To sacrifice His life,
to be hung on a tree.
His death had a purpose
for you and for me.
But death could not keep Him
bound up in the grave.
He rose up victorious,
from death He can save.

From the beginning,
when God called us "man".
To show us His love
was always His plan.
He died to save us
and set us apart.
He wants us to seek Him
with all of our heart.
We have the power
to overcome death.
When our life is filled with
His Holy Spirit's breath!

This is the story
that I like to hear.
It always reminds me
that I need not fear.
His love from beginning
will last to the end.
His love draws me to Him
and calls me His friend.
A friend to this sinner
is what He has been.
So I long for heaven,
I don't know just when.

I was in the middle of sweeping floors, cleaning, and singing to God when this poem filled my mind. One of my favorite hymns is "I Love To Tell the Story" but I'm not even sure if that is what I was singing when this poem showed up. I had to stop and type it out so I could go back to cleaning and singing. I pray that this ministers in the way God desires for it to and that it brings glory to His name.

Prayer Points

- Pray that God would fill you with a boldness to tell the story of His work in your life.

- Pray that you would not make light of the seriousness of sin.

- Pray with thanksgiving that God provided a sacrifice for your sin through His Son, Jesus.

- Pray that the people around you today would come to know and accept the story of Jesus as true and applicable to their life.

Stuck

I sit at my desk
with a poem that is stuck.
It started to form,
then it froze in the muck.
But that is okay,
no reason to fret.
I keep listening to God,
He's not done with me yet.
The poems aren't the real gift,
this now I see.
God's using them greatly
as He calls to me.

God is the author
who puts poems in my mind.
He calls me to Himself
to see what I find.
This gift He has given,
so what should I do.
I'll collect them and type them
and share them with you.
God likes to give good gifts,
these poems I received.
If you had just told me,
I may not have believed.

The real gift is greater
and it's not only mine.
To seek God's face always
is the gift that's quite fine.
I pray that you seek Him
and gaze on His face.
Enjoy the warmth always
of His loving embrace.
And as you do listen
on how you should live.
You'll find that God loves you
and to you He does give.

So when you consider
the things that you've got.
Don't think they're your doing,
of course, they are not.
Spend time with Jesus
as you examine His gift.
Then look all around you
to find someone to lift.
For the gifts God has given,
quite out of the blue.
Are meant to serve others
and not just for you.

That is my story
as I sit here at home.
I need not be worried
if my mind has no poem.
If my mind's filled with Jesus,
then that is the best.
If the poems do keep coming,
I pray that you're blest.
To share these poems with you,
still seems kind of odd.
But when I am giving,
I'm more like my God.

I had a poem start to form in my mind but when I went out to clear the driveway, it's as if it just froze somewhere in there. When I came in and tried to "thaw it out", I kept thinking about getting stuck. We don't like getting stuck because it means, or at least feels like, we're not going anywhere. God reminded me that even when I'm stuck He is there and He is more important than any gift or ability He has given. I pray that you actively seek God's face during the times you feel stuck.

Prayer Points

- Pray that you would be very careful not to make a gift God has placed in your life a substitute for God's presence in your life.

- Pray that you would constantly recognize, and credit, God as the author and giver of all the gifts and abilities you have.

- Pray that you would seek God to understand His purpose for the gifting He has put in your life.

- Pray that God's Spirit would give you direction in how He would have you share the gifts God has given.

- Pray that God would remove from your life all hints of selfishness that keeps you from sharing with others the good things God has given you.

- Pray for a Spirit-filled wisdom to help you be a wise steward of what you have been given.

- Pray that you would find contentment in accepting that God is enough even if the gifts and abilities you value would disappear.

- Pray that the people around you today would have a clearer picture of who Jesus is because of the way you use the things He has given you.

- Pray that God would fill you with the courage to do what He calls you to regardless of where it fits, or doesn't fit, into your comfort zone.

Survivor

We add and we tally,
we count all our things.
Perhaps if we have enough
we could be kings.
We say that we don't want
all that there is.
We only want more than
he would call his.
This cold fascination
becomes very odd.
When all we desire
is to simply be God.

My goal is quite simple
when I'm living large.
I don't care what you need
just put me in charge!
I'm more important
than all who you know.
Just ask and I'll tell you,
it really is so.
My goal is to out wit,
out last, and out play.
To step on all others
each and every day.

This does not sound right,
I'm really quite sure.
To live like the world,
God would not call pure.
So I'll re-examine
and make a fresh start.
God doesn't look outside,
He looks in my heart.
If it's full of darkness
and evil desire.
God fills it with His light
and cleanses with fire.

He calls me to look at
the way I do measure.
And to chase after boldly
the things He calls treasure.
To climb heaven's ladder
is different you see.
It's all about Jesus
and what Christ did for me.
And so I do tally
and measure and add.
Not for my own good –
it's all for my Dad!

Yep, another night hanging out with God and He shows me another poem that He had put in my head. I pray that this is a help and encouragement to whoever God brought it out for — even if that is only me.

Prayer Points

- Pray that God would help you to accurately evaluate both what you have and the purpose for which you have it.

- Pray that God's Spirit would convict you of any hint of greed that may be in your life that makes you seek your good above that of others.

- Pray that the time you spend with God in His Word would purify and cleanse you from all impure and evil desires.

- Pray that you would better understand that in God's perspective the servant is at the top of the ladder of success.

Teamwork

It is such a joy
to work with this team.
I pray that it's real,
and not just a dream.
Yes, there are times
that I work the day through.
But times I take Susan
and go to the zoo.
The freedom I have
is all built on trust.
It's not just important,
it's really a must.

As I look around
at these gals and guys.
To have a great team
should be no surprise.
They all are quite gifted
in doing their part.
The thing that is special,
is they serve from the heart.
No idea's better
just because of a name.
We want to be servants
not seeking our fame.

The thing that's surprising
and really quite sad.
This type of teamwork
is rare, like a fad.
If you think it's passing,
as fads often do.
Consider the value
of this team to you.
We do our best work,
or so it would seem.
When we work together
and act like a team.

> To seek good for others
> above all our own.
> Is the life of a servant
> that Jesus has shown.
> To not be afraid
> to do what it takes.
> Whether lofty or low,
> no difference it makes.
> It is such a blessing
> when help I can give.
> The joy is compounded
> when this way we live.

As I was finishing up the cleaning of the church building tonight and thinking about all the people who help and encourage me, God gave me this poem. I share it in honor of the Deer Run team who have made me feel like a valuable part of what God is doing through each of us. I pray that God continues to pour out His blessing on the work that He is doing through Deer Run.

Prayer Points

- Pray that God would help you to see the value of the people that He has brought into your life, and you into theirs.

- Pray that you would have a great appreciation for how God has gifted each part of the body differently in order to accomplish His purposes.

- Pray that you would have a right opinion of yourself and be willing to serve others and experience the joy of helping them know value.

Time With God

I listen to God
as I spend time in prayer.
It's hard to imagine,
why this seems so rare.
I have a great privilege
to talk to the King.
He calls to me softly,
everything I should bring.
He understands me
when others do not.
When I need to unload,
He'll take what I've got.

His kind, gentle whisper
is spoken so true.
I love you so fully,
my best is for you.
He's not like those others
whose promises fail.
When things are the hardest,
He never will bail.
He'll stand right beside me,
we'll walk hand in hand.
He says, "I am with you,
just see what I've planned."

That is the hard part,
to see what's not here.
To trust He'll deliver,
when I'm filled with fear.
He is so gracious,
so loving and kind.
He calms all my fears,
gives me peace of mind.
Every step forward,
I learn to trust more.
So that I am ready,
when He opens the door.

I don't always look for,
a door open wide.
For most of the time I
am comfortable inside.
Those are the times that,
He calls out to me.
"I'll never leave you,
step out here and see."
As He calls me forward,
I step out the door.
It's all I imagined
and oh, so much more.

As this keeps on happening,
again and again.
My trust builds up layers,
it's no longer thin.
While it is not perfect,
my listening has built.
A life with more freedom,
and a whole lot less guilt.
I know that God loves me
and works for my best.
Of this I am so sure,
that in Him I can rest.

So what will you do,
with the truth you have heard?
Will you take it to heart,
seeking God in His word?
When you walk in faith,
one step at a time.
He demands your all,
but it's worth every dime.
And as you surrender
and learn to just wait.
You'll find you are ready,
when you reach His gate.

I was spending time with God this afternoon and as I was waiting for an evening meeting, God reminded me of some of the wonderful destinations that He has taken me to as a result of my listening and following Him. In the midst of my worship of Him for His great love and faithfulness, He gave me this poem. I pray that it encourages you to spend more time with God.

Prayer Points

- Pray that you would realize the value of spending time with God on a regular basis.

- Pray that you would grasp more fully the desire that God has for you to spend time with Him.

- Pray that you would be filled with an overwhelming trust of God that allows you to be transparent with Him.

- Pray that the time you spend with God would refresh you in a way that you eagerly desire to be in His presence.

- Pray that the people around you would be drawn to spending greater amounts of time with God as they see the value it has in your life.

- Pray that you would not allow failures to derail your plans to spend regular time with God.

- Pray that you come to know God so well as you spend time with Him that it changes how you live.

Trouble

You will have trouble,
of this I am sure.
The question remaining,
how will you endure?
The good news of Jesus
says you're not alone.
He will be with you,
you don't need to phone.

Just call out to Jesus
in the midst of your fear.
He's always listening
and He'll always hear.
He won't forsake you,
as others may do.
He gives you His Spirit
to live inside you.

So when you have trouble,
just go to your knee.
Cry out to Jesus,
it sure works for me.
He may not remove you
from the midst of the mess.
But He'll carry you through,
to that I confess.

I've been reflecting on life experiences and the words of Jesus in my listening times with God recently. I think that we must either completely miss, or simply ignore, the words of Jesus when He tells us we will have trouble. This poem came out of thinking about our need to expect, and be ready for, trouble.

In prayer,
Tom

Prayer Points

- Pray not that God would remove you from times of trouble, but that God would grow you through times of trouble.

- Pray for a steadfastness of spirit that will help you endure the difficult times of trouble that Jesus said would come our way as His followers.

- Pray that the people around you would see your faith and your faithfulness when they observe how you handle trouble.

- Pray that God's Spirit would constantly remind you of His presence and His promise to never leave you nor forsake you.

- Pray that God would protect you from giving in to the temptations that often come in times of hardship and trouble.

- Pray that you would allow the power of Jesus in your life to remove any remnants of pride that would keep you from turning to Him in your times of need.

- Pray that your times of trouble are dealt with between you and God and don't become fuel for gossip and criticism of others.

- Pray that you would reach out to others and help them to carry their burdens during their times of trouble.

Truth

It's cold and it's snowy
outside of the door.
But I'm warm and cozy,
asleep on the floor.
I know what you're saying,
that you'd like to see.
Asleep and still writing
that just can not be.
It may not seem likely –
it may not seem real.
I'm only sharing
the things that I feel.

If you just don't like it,
that's fine with me.
You can do something useful,
like watch "reality" TV!
It's really not funny
the things we accept.
As true and important
though the facts are inept.
We read and we study,
we search through the 'net.
To prove what we want to,
and the rest we forget.

As my mind does wander,
and goes to and fro.
I consider what's in it
and I think of the snow.
It doesn't matter
if I say it is hot.
I can say it forever,
but still, it is not.
The point to this story,
is about to come.
I can't make my own truth,
It comes from the Son!

Okay, I went out to clear the snow from the driveway at home and another poem fell out of my head. I pray that this reaches the person God intended for it to reach.

In prayer,
Tom Lemler

Prayer Points

- Pray that you would look to Jesus and the Word of God as the source for all truth.

- Pray that God's Spirit would closely guard your heart and mind from accepting, and retelling, anything that is false.

- Pray for a spirit of discernment to be able to understand when things that are presented as truth are not.

- Pray that you would be more concerned about the integrity of God's Word than about you being right about everything.

- Pray that the people around you today would know you as a person that speaks truth.

- Pray for the humility to be able to admit when you are wrong.

- Pray for a spirit of understanding and forgiveness when others turn out to be wrong about things that they believed to be true.

Warnings

I have a computer
that's trying to die.
I open a program
and it asks me, "Why?".
"This will cause problems,
for my memory is low."
"I warned you this time;
so yes, I'll be slow."
"If you do not heed
this helpful advice."
"I'll shut myself down,
I won't warn you twice."

The brain can be like
this computer of mine.
When it functions well,
everything does just shine.
But let it fill up
with unhealthy stuff.
And it isn't long
before it's running rough.
Add to the problem
some unrelenting stress.
And before very long,
the whole thing's a mess.

Just like the computer,
a warning we get.
The body calls out,
"I'm here, don't forget."
But so very often,
when we ache and much more.
The warnings God gives us,
we simply ignore.
Ignore it for too long,
I say with a frown.
It could be disaster,
as your body shuts down.

So what do I do
for my computer and me?
When things are not right
and the warnings I see.
I look to the manual
and seek to restore.
The purpose and function,
I was created for.
I clear out all garbage
and cleanse from within.
I restore a memory
that is free from all sin.

I trim down my files
to what's needed most.
I only have room,
for good things to host.
I empty my mind
of things from the past.
And only hold on to,
that which should last.
It's an ongoing process,
not done in a day.
It's a daily surrender
to God and His Way.

If you've not noticed,
the subject is me.
It's not really about
the computer, you see.
The warnings God gives me,
I need to observe.
So I function smoothly
as His name I serve.
I pray that you notice,
the warnings in you.
So you would be faithful
as you serve Him too.

My computer has been giving me warning messages and randomly stopping off and on for a few days. In addition to that, I've had a headache for much of the day and the work going on in the building hasn't helped much. As I took some time to rest and listen to God prior to a meeting tonight, He put this poem in my mind. I pray that it serves His purposes and brings Him glory.

Prayer Points

- Pray that you would pay attention to the warnings that God brings into your life.

- Pray that you would allow God's Spirit to examine your life and reveal any junk that is hindering your effectiveness.

- Pray for forgiveness and restoration from any specific sin that is in your life.

- Pray that you would fill your life with the things of God as you replace all that needs removed from your life.

- Pray that the people around you today would be willing to heed the warnings that God would bring into their lives.

- Pray that you would set aside time to spend with God to listen for the warnings that He is speaking into your life.

- Pray that God would fill you with wisdom, courage, and direction in responding to the warnings that you experience.

Why

These poems just keep coming,
I'm not for sure why.
They show up complete,
I don't really try.
While listening to God,
they appear in my mind.
It's not like I'm writing,
it's more like I find.
I think that His purpose
is more than just one.
They help me, they help you,
sometimes they're just fun.

When you are discouraged
and doubting God's care.
Draw near as you trust Him
and know that He's there.
Perhaps He will show you
in a way that is new.
His gifts and His mercy
each day are for you.
And if you don't get
something you feel's unique.
Don't worry about it
if God's face you still seek.

Just use what He gives you
in the way that you should.
Reach out and help others,
every day do some good.
God isn't worried
if you can do what I do.
And He doesn't call me
to be just like you.
So please be encouraged
with just who you are.
If your home is in heaven,
you're bound to go far!

Since these poems began showing up in my head a month ago, I've been asking myself "Why?" and "Why now?". I suppose God gave me this one tonight as part of the answers to those questions. I used to do quite a bit of short, devotional writing and really felt closely connected to God's Spirit when we would work on those. Then I went through a stretch of time where it often didn't seem like I had time to breathe, let alone spend needed time with God. I think the poems are a new thing to make sure I recognize that this is God's gift and not simply a return to something that I thought I was good at. I pray that you recognize and acknowledge God's gifting in your life, then use it for His glory.

Prayer Points

- Pray that you would learn contentment in accepting that some of the work of God is meant to be a mystery.

- Praise God for extending His grace and mercy to you because of His great love.

- Pray that your not having a full understanding of the workings of God would not keep you from using the things that He gives you.

- Pray that God would help you to avoid the comparison trap that keeps you from enjoying the gifts He has given.

- Pray that you would use God's gifts in your life for His glory even when you're not completely sure why He gave them to you.

Words

Words can be powerful,
more than we know.
For good or for bad,
either way it can go.
A careless word spoken
is striking a spark.
Then the mind quickly takes us
to a place that is dark.
Over and over
the mind plays a word.
And after a while
nothing else can be heard.

I think far too often
our tongue starts to say.
Things that are hurtful
and get in the way.
Words come between us
when freely they flow.
We don't stop to think,
so out the mouth they do go.
If you're not so certain
of all of these claims.
Then pick up a Bible,
read the words penned by James.

And while this sounds hopeless
and out of control.
Words can bring healing
and help make you whole.
A word fitly spoken
is like an apple of gold.
A word that brings healing
is a thing to behold!
The Word that is Jesus
is quite a big deal.
A word from the Savior
has the power to heal.

So as you consider
the words that you use.
The ones that bring healing,
I pray you do choose.
The ones that are careless
and bring such great hurt.
I pray you remove them
along with the dirt.
And as you spread good things
by what you do say.
I pray that God's Spirit
brings great healing today.

This is one of three poems that rolled out of my head in rather quick succession as I spent time listening to God for direction and peace. I pray that these words are of the healing kind in your life and mine.

Prayer Points

- Pray that God would place a guard over your tongue to keep careless words from flying out of your mouth.

- Pray that the words you use would be helpful for the building up and encouragement of others.

- Pray that God would fill you with wisdom in knowing both what and when to speak.

- Pray that the people around you today would experience the healing power of the words of life that come from God's Word.

Work Day

The sun's shining brightly
so out I do go.
For somebody has to
shovel all of this snow.
I know most are tired
of feeling they're stuck.
So I head out the door
and start up my truck.
To have all things ready,
at least I do pray.
Should schools not be closed
for at least one more day.

Nearly everything in the area had closed down for a couple of days due to snow and extreme cold for the second time in the month. As the state of emergency was lifted, I needed to get to work and make sure the building was ready should it be decided to go back to school the next day. This was a poem that it seemed like God gave me just for fun but I share it anyhow so He can use it as He pleases.

Prayer Points

- Pray that you would serve God with a sense of joy and contentment, knowing that the labor you do in His name is not done in vain.

- Pray that God would fill you with His peace in the midst of the simple things of life.

- Pray that your work would be a benefit to you and would be done as one who is serving the Lord.

Work In Progress

The poems keep on coming,
that God gives to me.
Their purpose is shrouded
in some mystery.
As I consider,
the things God has done.
It seems they have reason,
that's more than just fun.
This gift that He gave me,
He calls me to share.
So you can glimpse Jesus
and know of His care.

It happened so quickly,
it caught me off guard.
If I tried to write these,
it would be quite hard.
It may not be writing,
but collecting I do.
The poems that God gives me,
I do share with you.
The stories within them,
I hope you do see.
Are stories of Jesus,
how He's worked in me.

There are still times that
I sit on the fence.
So God's working in me
is still present tense.
I was asked a question,
I had no answer for.
So I sought God fully
and He gave me more.
It is in times of quiet
and seeking God's face.
He makes Himself known
and gives me this grace.

He does remind me,
it says in His Word.
That people won't know Him,
unless they have heard.
And people won't hear Him,
unless I will go.
And tell of His goodness,
I already know.
To put His great message,
in words such as these.
So someone might read them,
and God seek to please.

And while it's amazing,
the response that has come.
I pray that He'll use,
these words to reach some.
To encourage someone,
or brighten a day.
Perhaps show a person
that God knows the way.
To challenge a reader,
to look deep within.
And get rid of all things
that could lead to sin.

To help people realize
there's a God that does care.
No matter where you're at,
up close or out there.
I've been to those places,
at times in my life.
He's been in my good times,
and walked me through strife.
Whatever you have done,
He calls out to you.
Come walk beside me,
I'll make all things new.

I was spending time with God this afternoon resting my mind, spirit, and body when a bunch of rhyming thoughts filled my mind. As I tried to sort it all out, this was the result. I pray that it gives you a glimpse of God's work in me and that it encourages you to allow God to work in you, even in unexpected ways.

Prayer Points

- Pray that you would recognize the ongoing work of God in your life.

- Pray that you would seek God's direction in using the gifts He gives you -- even when you may not see clearly the purpose He is using them for.

- Pray that you would be filled with humility as you continually point people to God as the source of all of the good work that is in progress in your life.

- Pray that you would be faithful in using the work God is doing in you to share the message of salvation with others.

- Pray that your recognition of God's work in you still being in progress would help you to have a greater understanding of others who are also in progress.

- Pray that you would not give up on God's continual work in your life.

- Pray that the people around you would allow God to begin a work in progress in their life.